*The Art of*

# FALLING
# IN LVE

# The Art of
# FALLING
## IN L♥VE

## JOE BEAM

**HOWARD BOOKS**
A DIVISION OF SIMON & SCHUSTER, INC.
New York • Nashville • London • Toronto • Sydney • New Delhi

Howard Books
A Division of Simon & Schuster, Inc.
1230 Avenue of the Americas
New York, NY 10020

First Howard Books trade paperback edition January 2013

HOWARD and colophon are trademarks of Simon & Schuster, Inc.

For information about special discounts for bulk purchases, please contact
Simon & Schuster Special Sales at
1-866-506-1949 or business@simonandschuster.com.

The Simon & Schuster Speakers Bureau can bring authors to your live event.
For more information or to book an event, contact the
Simon & Schuster Speakers Bureau at
1-866-248-3049 or visit our website at www.simonspeakers.com.

Designed by Ruth Lee-Mui

Illustrations by Randy Drake

Manufactured in the United States of America

1   3   5   7   9   10   8   6   4   2

The Library of Congress has cataloged the hardcover edition as follows:

Beam, Joe.
The art of falling in love / Joe Beam.
p. cm.
1. Man-woman relationships. 2. Love. 3. Mate selection. 4. Interpersonal relations. I. Title.
HQ801.B352 2012
302.3—dc23
2011036615

ISBN 978-1-4516-4933-8
ISBN 978-1-4516-7265-7 (pbk)
ISBN 978-1-4516-4944-4 (ebook)

*For Alice,*
*my companion on the LovePath*

# Contents

# *Preface*

*This is a* book about love.

It comes from my heart and personal experience, and is based on social and medical science as well as many years of success in guiding people to the deepest levels of love. As part of my work in the field of love, I study research from scholars, marriage experts, and love experts and examples around the world. As I worked through graduate studies in clinical psychology, I read widely on the topic. I spent several years studying romantic attachment and its challenges. I even dug into the passionate part of marriage by enrolling in a PhD program at the University of Sydney in Australia, one of the world's most prestigious centers of learning. I have worked with and read from some of the most learned thinkers of our time in the emerging science of why human beings fall in love, why they fall out of love, and how they fall in love again.

More important, I have learned about love from working with thousands of people, singles and married couples, some happily married and some who had already filed for divorce. More than 100,000 people have enrolled in my courses, workshops, and seminars. I've spoken to millions more on programs such as NBC's *Today* Show, ABC's *Good Morning America*, and *Focus on the Family*. And I've shared what I've learned through books and articles.

All of which isn't to blow my horn, but to show that the concepts, models, and explanations about love—how to fall in love, how to stay in love, and how to fall in love all over again—have been tested in real lives of real people over many years. Some of their stories are in this book, though the identities of individuals are hidden and stories are composites of many people's experiences. To those of you who have attended one of my workshops, rest easy—you won't find your story here. No story is shared exactly as it happened with any one person or couple.

The truths are genuine and valid.

The stories are vases in which I display those truths.

As with any book, this work involved many people. Don Black and David Byerley are both friends who helped me get this project off the ground. Rob Suggs is the wordsmith who helped me develop the initial version of this book faster than I could have alone.

Of course, without my wife, Alice, I would know little to nothing about true love. She loves when others would abandon. The same is true of my children, Angela, Joanna, and Kimberly. No husband or father has ever been loved more. Joanna gives that same level of love to her husband, Lee Wilson. Kimberly does so with her husband, Rob Holmes.

If you wish to know what love is, this book will be your guide. If you desire a love that is sane and rational, yet full of never-ending emotion, you will find the path to that love here. You *will* learn the art of falling in love.

# WELCOME
# TO THE
# LOVEPATH

# THE PATH TO LOVE

"*No one who* knows them believes that this marriage can make it. I am not exaggerating. No one."

My orthodontist continued adjusting my latter-life braces while explaining all he knew about his friend's marriage. Their story matched so many others. Names and locales differed, but the basics remained the same. She had an affair. He retaliated with an affair of his own. Hers was brief, accompanied by intense guilt and a strong desire to restore her marriage. His was not. It evolved from a vengeful fling to an intense craving to be with his new paramour for the rest of his life.

"I can help. I'd say the odds are three out of four that I can help them fall in love again."

That's what I wanted to say, but his hands were in my mouth. When he finally gave me a rest, I spoke the words with a quiet confidence born of experience with thousands of couples. My orthodontist's reaction was not nearly as confident, but he was intrigued enough that he asked me to explain.

I told him about the LovePath. What it is. How it works for people who are single or married. Why it can change the course of lives, even when that seems impossible. I concluded by asking him to use his influence to get his friends to come to a Marriage Helper weekend workshop, sessions geared specifically for couples in crisis. I promised him that I would make a personal appearance to present the section on the LovePath and to meet his friends. I told him that it made no difference if they wanted to save the marriage or not; if they attended the workshop, we still had a 75 percent chance of saving the marriage, even if one or both wanted the marriage over. "Put all the pressure you can on them. Just get them there."

He did.

They came.

In that weekend, the husband began to understand love as he never had before. He gained insight into himself and where his current path was taking him. He discovered a different path altogether, and for the first time in years had a glimpse of what true love could be.

The workshop did not reduce the intense passion he felt for his lover, but it opened the door for a rather remarkable life change. Because he lived near me, I agreed to meet with him weekly as he worked through understanding himself, his emotions, and his future. Slowly, he started on the LovePath, but with his wife now rather than with the other woman.

*"I am more in love with my wife than I ever thought possible. We will love each other more every day as long as we live."*

His wife focused on the LovePath as well, doing what we taught to make love grow.

How did it turn out? If you ever see the ninety-minute DVD made to accompany this book, you will meet them on your TV screen. Not only did they follow the LovePath to fall deeply in love with each other, he now volunteers to help other couples do the same. As he said a few days before I wrote this chapter, "I am more in love with my wife than I ever thought possible. We will love each other more every day as long as we live." She stood beside him, saying the same words, smiling.

They will be in love forever.

# I CAN HELP YOU FALL IN LOVE

I help people fall in love.

Sometimes I help singles learn the path of love so that they can find and savor the love of their dreams. I help couples who crave more in their marriages to fall in love more deeply. I show the lonely, alienated, or hurt how to fall in love all over again when they have misplaced their love and cannot find it anymore.

I will show you how to have the love you want.

No, there is nothing magic or special about me. It's just that I know love. As with most of us, I have learned through personal experiences—both good and bad—but I have also learned from social and medical science, which I study constantly. Most important, I have learned from working with tens of thousands of couples and guiding them successfully through a process that creates, deepens, or restores love.

This process is the LovePath.

# THE MOST WONDERFUL RUMOR

If I were to ask several great philosophers to define the meaning of life, I imagine I would receive a variety of responses, from the religious to the philosophical. However, most of the answers, regardless of their complexity, would ultimately have something to do with that simplest of words, the idea that launched ten thousand pop songs and old movies, and the quest that every world religion ultimately embraces: *love*.

As human beings, we have needs that scientists can explain and quantify:

We need a breath of oxygen every couple of seconds.
We need water every few hours.
We need food every day, and we need shelter every night.

These are the simple physical requirements of survival. However, we need love and acceptance, too. Once those more basic survival needs are taken care of, we spend most of our lives searching to fulfill the great desire that satisfies the soul—the experience of love.

This thing we all want so badly doesn't cost a dime, yet the pure form we seek is more precious than gold. I am speaking, of course, about what we might call "true love." Because you are a human being, I believe you know exactly what I am talking about.

Of course, there is bad love. I imagine you could tell some stories about your own experiences with this. If bad love could be cashed in at the bank, we would all be very wealthy.

However, true love is another thing entirely. None of us wants to compromise on the quality of love that we get out of life. We want love that overpowers, that sweeps us off our feet.

So how do we get our hands on it?

Some people believe there is no such thing. They say that as long as people themselves cannot be true, there can be no true love. Sure, most of these cynics have fallen head-over-heels in love, just like everyone else. But as often as not, after love fails, people decide that maybe it was all an illusion, a hormonal hiccup, a biological itch that had to be scratched. A passing fancy after some fancy passes. Love comes, the skeptics say, and then it goes. It's simply too good to last.

Others believe that love exists, but that it's a mysterious force, a powerful, roaming emotion with a mind of its own. It is a viral infection of passion that we catch for a while only to lose. This thing called love, they claim, is no more within our control than an asteroid plummeting from outer space to flatten us on the sidewalk. Love is mercurial. After all, you didn't hire Cupid, and neither did your mate. The little winged fellow flew out from behind a bush one day and fired a couple arrows your way, like in the cartoons. The trouble, according to this myth, is that the narcotic on the tip of those arrows is temporary. It wears off, and there's nothing you can do about it.

Ask some of the Hollywood stars who are regulars in the gossip columns; the narcotic on some of their arrows apparently lasts no more than two or three weeks.

So there are those who say true love does not exist, and those who say true love does not endure.

But for some reason, those of us who have known love can't believe the critics, can we? Because for all the bad love we've endured, observed, and heard about, rumors persist of something that is not bad love at all, of something real and wonderful. Just when we think love has gone completely out of style, we run into some stubborn instance of a sincere, genuine, and powerful love. Have you ever seen an elderly couple like that? Say, two octogenarians as fully devoted to each other as they were half a century ago? These two do not just tolerate each other but absolutely dote upon each other. No, I am not talking about the gentleness and politeness common to many seniors. I'm talking about a very obvious passion between two ordinary human beings— a passion that has endured and even grown stronger, year by year. A passion that keeps the life and light shining in their eyes even in their declining years.

But real love is not confined to some past generation. There are couples out there who enjoy a fabulous and fulfilling love relationship every day. Do they ever bicker? Absolutely. Do they act like love-struck teenagers who are obsessed with each other? Nope, we are not talking about hearts-and-flowers stuff, but mature, fully developed love that makes better human beings out of everyone who finds it.

Interested in learning about that kind of love, and the path to find it? Keep reading.

## GETTING ON THE RIGHT TRACK

Years ago, I began to ask serious questions about this mysterious human experience of love. I had a life history that raised serious questions in my mind and spirit. I could see my life as a twisting path from childhood to adolescence to adulthood.

I wondered how I fell in love, how I fell out of it, and if I could ever fall in love again.

As a young man, my path intersected with that of another human being, Alice, who eventually became my wonderful wife. She was heading somewhere in life, based on her identity, her needs, and her goals. I was heading somewhere else, based on my own. We felt a mutual *attraction*, which is the first stage of the romantic experience. I bought into everything about Alice that I experienced with her—her identity, her needs, and her goals as I understood them. (Pay close attention to that last phrase; in time we will have much more to say about it.) Alice bought into the totality of what she encountered in Joe Beam. What we experienced is the event of *mutual acceptance*.

Then, after connecting in such a fulfilling way, the emotional narcotic kicked in. There were joy, excitement, and that thrill that comes like a great wave and washes two people toward the impulse to become life partners. This is *attachment*.

All of these stages are standard. I could be telling the story of millions of people. But then comes the intersection of another factor: time. The passage of time changes nearly everything in its path. Including love.

*Why was love so wonderful to find, yet so hard to maintain?*

With the passage of time, my passion began to waver. What, I wondered, happened to me? Why had the road in my journey grown so difficult? Why was love so wonderful to find, yet so hard to maintain? I loved loving Alice; she loved loving me. Why did the "drug" wear off? Had it all been an illusion? Could we get back what we had had? Did we even want to?

After fifteen years of marriage, I entered a period of my life that was painful beyond belief. Alice and I divorced. I lost my sense of who I was, wounding Alice and myself in the process. In time I found my way back onto the path—not just the path of being committed to a relationship but also the path of making that relationship really work. After three years of divorce, Alice and I married each other again. I am here to tell you that it was not easy or neat to do so. It took personal growth, understanding, perseverance—and a few swift kicks to my rear, among other things.

Here's what I discovered: There is a way. A starting point. A direction. A strategy to get to where we wanted to be. The power of love is *not* some mysterious extra-human emotional force whose mysteries and staying power are beyond our control. It is no simple itch that needs scratching. (Can you think of any "itch" that can wound us so deeply—or that feels so good when we scratch it right?)

No, what I discovered is a journey that I began to call the LovePath. Every single one of us has the opportunity to travel this road of self-understanding, interpersonal bonding, and ultimate gratification. Best of all, it's a way of living that we intentionally and proactively choose, rather than passively gain and lose. On this path, anyone can find and experience love, relationships can be built to last, and relationships can be rescued if they fail. The LovePath is the most hopeful, exhilarating message I know, so I have devoted my life to telling people about it. Those who understand and follow it master the art of falling in love.

I work with thousands of people, both single and married, who are wanting to start the path, are somewhere on that path, or are stranded by the side of the road. In helping so many ordinary, struggling people understand the different stages of the LovePath, in helping them learn the art of falling and staying in love, I have seen miracles take place. We have been able to help lovers build relationships that work and keep working. On the part of the path that constitutes marriage, we have helped thousands upon thousands of couples reach levels of love they never expected to find. Perhaps even more fascinating, we have a record of accomplishment of saving three out of four crisis marriages— marriages on the brink of ending when the couple attended our Marriage Helper seminar.

I see the light go on in people's eyes as they understand their journey for the first time. Moreover, I know they want to make it, that they'll find the happiness they've always wanted.

This approach works; I have seen it. I have lived its success myself, and I have the scars to prove what happens when we stray from the path. I have been interviewed on many radio and TV programs to share the keys of a healthy, thriving, and fulfilling relationship.

Now I look forward to sharing those keys with you.

## WHAT IS LOVE?

Dr. Robert Sternberg, provost and senior vice president at Oklahoma State University, developed a model for understanding love that is found in *Cupid's Arrow*, one of more than sixty books he has written. To understand love, Sternberg divides it into its three basic components: intimacy, commitment, and passion.

These are not the steps of the LovePath, but rather results of following the LovePath. They are what we seek in true love, and the Love-Path brings them into existence for us. Before beginning the path, let's explore what Dr. Sternberg and others have learned about the dimensions of the love we so want and need.

### Intimacy

Intimacy is closeness, warmth, and the feeling of being bonded together. When men hear the word, they tend to think of it as something they do. Women, on the other hand, think of it as something they feel.

*Intimacy is being transparent, building trust, and allowing another to look deep into your soul.*

Intimacy is truly knowing one another or, taking the very sound of the word, *into-me-see*. Intimacy is being transparent, building trust, and allowing another to look deep into your soul. Intimacy means giving respect, developing deep friendship, and connecting on a level that words never reach.

Without intimacy, true love cannot exist. Yet intimacy is one of the most difficult things to master because to achieve it, two individuals must allow their souls to go naked before each other, ensuring that their love is for the real person—not a picture the person has painted. When one feels intimacy with another, she feels that the other is a friend in the deepest and most meaningful sense of the word. He is one who knows her as she truly is, not as she represents herself in different environments and situations. He sees her weaknesses, flaws, or failures yet continues to believe the best about her. He understands her deepest desires, her dreams, and her fanciful wishes—even those she would be embarrassed for anyone else to know.

He knows what she is afraid of, what she will fight for, and, perhaps, die for. He is aware of her consistencies and her inconsistencies, but never bothers to catalog either. He cares about what she wanted to be when she grew up and understands her feelings about what she became instead.

Her secrets are safe with him. Her love. Her total being. She never thinks of the possibility of his betrayal. She knows that he loves her deeply and completely, that he will never leave her, that he would search the earth over for her if she went missing.

If she were in danger, he would protect her. It would not matter whether she was right or wrong; he would never abandon her. He would sacrifice himself for her in battle, even if the battle was one she was wrong to have started.

He sees into her soul.

Soul mate, you say?

No. That phrase is too trite. A truly intimate relationship is one that exists in the deepest regions of our being, one that is essential to our innermost sense of worth and to our need for security in an insecure world. It is not just a friendship. It reaches the depths. It is oneness.

It is the purest form of love.

Not only do most of us crave this kind of love and relationship, we must have it to feel complete. It is the strongest need within us after our need for physical survival—and sometimes it transcends that.

Not long before writing this, I received another letter underscoring this universal desire for intimacy. This particular letter came from a young woman who had recently ended an affair and was struggling to put her marriage back together. She intensely desired to earn her husband's trust and fall in love with him all over again. No matter how much they worked at it, she was not developing the same level of emotional bridging with him as she had with her former paramour.

> *I'm not chasing some kind of sexual thrill. I don't even care if I have sex at ALL! I need a man who will look inside me, know me, understand me, and love me. But the only way my husband knows how to communicate right now is to have sex. It's like he's reclaiming his territory or something. Like he's trying to prove he can be better than . . . well, you know who I'm referring to. Why can't he understand that the affair wasn't about sex? It was about two people bonding and being totally open to each other. That's what I want. It's what I have to have.*
>
> *But that is NOT happening! With my husband, I have to disguise, hide, and whitewash my true feelings. He just can't accept me as I am. I do not want to continue in this marriage if to get his love I have to pretend to be somebody that I'm not. How am I supposed to fall in love again with this man . . . this man I hurt so deeply and I want to love so badly [sic] . . . if he either can't or won't love the real me?*
>
> *Am I wrong to want this soul-to-soul, heart-to-heart level of love?*

No, she is not wrong. Her unfaithfulness did not remove her need or her right to have emotional intimacy with her husband. If he chooses to continue his marriage with her, not only will he need to find healing for his own hurt, but he also will have to help heal the hurt in her that made her vulnerable to unfaithfulness. He must understand her deep-felt need for intimacy and open himself to achieving oneness with her. That level of intimacy goes much deeper than having sex.

## Passion

Passion, too, is much more than sex. It is a craving for oneness with the other. Sexual passion subsides with the length of relationship, but *passion* can grow throughout a lifetime. It's the emotion you feel when you experience something wonderful—maybe a gorgeous sunset or an exciting event—and the first thought that springs to mind is the wish that your lover were with you to share it. This passion keeps love not only alive but also dynamic, and is even better when older than when young.

Love screams out for passion, for expressions of one's feelings in thought, word, and action. Lovers laugh together, sometimes loudly! Lovers feel free to whoop, holler, sing, dance, throw kisses, or just sit together on a swing in silence. They can fall at each other's feet or just watch the other sleep. Whatever they feel, they do not hide. They share more than their mutual existences; they share their hearts and their minds.

> *Whatever lovers feel, they do not hide. They share more than their mutual existences; they share their hearts and their minds.*

Isn't that what makes romance so exhilarating? Think of a young man passionately in love. He gets excited at the sight of his lover, thinks about her constantly when he is away from her, and sees her as the most beautiful girl in the world. He would rather be with her than anyone else and cannot imagine anyone making him as happy. Nothing is more important to him than his relationship with her. He adores her, cannot imagine life without her. Any thought of losing her creates immediate panic.

If you have experienced passion for your beloved, you know how wonderful it is—and how we relish the sensations of such intensely romantic love.

## Commitment

Commitment is the bedrock of love.

It is the decision to continue a relationship, to love someone, and maintain the love. It constitutes a measurement of how strongly we value our relationship. When one is committed to another, it means that we will always be there *with* the other person—no matter what—and *for* the other person.

Commitment keeps lovers together when life and its circumstances try to pull them apart. It gives safety and assurance. Committed lovers know that passing emotions are not a true gauge for the demise of their relationship. Commitment means that no matter what he feels as she walks out the door in the morning, he knows she is coming back. No pitfall, no person, no situation will be allowed to separate committed lovers.

We want the intimacy and passion that makes love magnificent, but we just as strongly want to know that our lover will be with us tomorrow—and for the thousand tomorrows after that. We want to know that the other person is with us through thick and thin. Good times and bad. When we deserve our lover and when we do not.

In a truly loving relationship, we have an unalterable need within us for absolute confidence that we both are committed to maintaining our relationship. We need to know without any doubt that neither of us will ever let another person or thing come between us. We need to be certain that our love for each other will last for the rest of our lives, and that our relationship will be stable. We need to know that each feels responsibility for the other. Moreover, that neither considers the possibility of the relationship ever ending.

Romantic love without commitment is like leaping from an airplane without a parachute. You may experience the most intense physical sensations and maximum emotions of your life, but it will end badly. Very, very badly.

## TRUE LOVE

You and I live in a strange world. On one hand, our culture is obsessed with love. Just look at the magazines at the checkout counter of your grocery store. What guiding themes do you see? The editors of the "glossies" are not fools. They know love sells. Why wouldn't it, with so many of us searching for answers about it?

On the other hand, our culture is confused about what love is. If we watch enough movies and TV shows and read enough issues of *People* magazine, we'll end up thinking that love is something that happens to Brad Pitt and Angelina Jolie and their red-carpet friends, that great love is the exclusive domain of physically beautiful people.

Then, if our image in the mirror is not Hollywood-class, we despair. We cannot help but notice that many of these dazzlingly gorgeous people cannot hang on to a relationship, even though they both are physical perfection! So what does that say about our chances with more "resistible" partners?

Then there is the *Playboy* magazine angle. That industry sells the sizzle of love as the sum of all body parts, surgically enhanced by doctors and manipulated to perfection by computer whizzes. Is that what love really is? A fantasy? In addition, if there are only so many female swimsuit models or male soap opera stars, are we doomed to experience some lesser, sub-foldout love? Can we be happy with someone who would never be a candidate for the Swimsuit Issue of *Sports Illustrated*?

I have some very good news for you. As difficult as it is to filter out the constant media messages that bombard us, we can know what real beauty is, and what genuine love feels like. You can have a relationship so wonderful that the glittering celebrities, if only they understood what you possessed, would give up all their looks for it. The fact is that every one of us can find genuine beauty in ourselves, the same in a life mate, and a mutually satisfying love that will endure forever, a love that hard times will only enhance and strengthen.

Are you ready to find out where you are on the LovePath? Are you ready to discover what the next phase of the journey holds for you?

## A PREVIEW OF THE LOVEPATH

Perhaps you want to know a little more about what lies ahead. After all, why should you read one more book about love and relationships? Well, here's a glimpse of what you will gain from reading *The Art of Falling in Love*.

First, I will give you the tools to understand the path you have already walked. As you do so, you will find yourself thinking, "That's exactly what happened to me! How did Joe know that?" You see, so much of our road is universal. So many of our obstacles are the same ones that everyone else faces, and for good reason. Scientific research is helping us understand the human experience more clearly than ever before, including romantic love. We'll explore together the latest findings about why you made certain decisions and felt certain feelings. You will learn amazing new truths about yourself.

Second, I will help you learn how to get what you want and need from love. As you come to know yourself and the LovePath better, you will better understand your needs and learn how to communicate them. When that happens, life and love bring you more fulfillment than you ever thought possible. Marriages on the edge, marriages in distress, will grow and deepen, becoming what the partners always longed for. Any already strong marriage or romantic relationship can become even stronger using the concepts we will discuss in this book.

Third, I will give you tools to learn how to overcome the past. Have you ever felt as if you were trying to walk uphill with a huge burden on your shoulders—and you could not seem to lay it down? Our life experiences cause us pain, damaged emotions, and unpleasant memories that we cannot seem to erase. I have been there myself. We *can* overcome the negative events of the past and experience life with a clean slate. There is no reason in the world that your past should be repeated in your future. This book shares the keys to letting go of those old burdens.

Fourth, I will help you learn how to fall in love the "right" way. If you already have a mate, you will discover how to fall in love all over again. I enjoy this aspect most. If you are single, the path will help you avoid common missteps. If you are married, you will learn how to make your marriage better. Even if your marriage has entered dangerous territory, you are going to find that miracles still occur—and that there is no reason one cannot happen for you. We can do much more than help you patch up old wounds with a Band-Aid so that you may grit your teeth and soldier on. We can show you how to reawaken the love you thought was lost forever and find a deep intimacy that is much more powerful and fulfilling than you ever had—or thought possible.

Does this sound like a journey you would like to travel?

Then come, let us begin the path.

### CHAPTER SUMMARY

Love is not some magical thing that suddenly appears or disappears. It is a process. Learn the process and you can use it to develop, deepen, or rescue true love.

*Love has three basic components:*
- Intimacy—openness and vulnerability to your lover
- Passion—a desire for true oneness with that person
- Commitment—doing what it takes to make the relationship last

*In* The Art of Falling in Love, *you will learn four things:*
- How to understand the path you've already walked
- How to get what you want and need from love
- How to overcome the past
- How to fall in love the "right" way—or fall in love all over again

If you are reading this book along with others, use the Group Discussion Guide at the end to gain greater insight.

# STEP ONE:
# ATTRACTION

# THE CALL TO
# CLOSENESS

*She looked like* a lost little girl. Slightly slumped, obviously afraid, with that faraway look in her eyes that made you want to hold her and assure her that everything was going to be all right. I could have done that because I believed it would be.

Lisa did not.

For her, life had taken a nasty turn and she felt no confidence about her future.

"What do you do when you're a thirty-six-year-old mother of two who's been abandoned by her husband for a twenty-two-year-old hard body? Look at me. I can't compete with those twenty-somethings. They don't have two kids under five; they don't have to come home from work and be Mommy all evening. They don't have to worry about having enough money. I'm going to be alone for the rest of my life, raising these boys by myself, and all this happens when I'm just thirty-six."

She struggled for control, then went on.

"I've seen that singles class at church with all the women who've been in it for years, hoping for a husband but not even finding a regular boyfriend. Is that what I'm going to be? A divorcée who longs for the attention of any man who will make me feel special, even for the evening. I don't want to live like that."

I could have explained to Lisa that she could find completeness without a man in her life, but that was not what she wanted to hear. Actually, she did not want to hear anything. She wanted to *be heard*. She wanted someone to know her pain, her fear, and, after hearing it all, to understand her anger. And her panic. She did not want to spend the rest of her life alone, just her and her sons. Like so many of us, she longed for a companion to love, and to love her. Part of her loathed that as a weakness and part of her did not care. She had given her love to a man who seemed to return it for years—until he tossed it out so he could love someone else. She felt she deserved a loving companion, but had no idea how to find him. Or, if she did find him, how to develop a mutual love. She even doubted she could find a man any better than the one who left her. Thankfully, she told me in no uncertain terms that she was not going to try to take one of the "good" ones who were already married. She would never be that woman.

*The most important thing to know about finding true love is that you must first love yourself.*

I did not give her advice during that encounter. However, a few weeks later, when she had calmed somewhat, I shared this with her: "Lisa, the most important thing to know about finding true love is that you must first love yourself. You have to believe in you. Who you are. What you are. How you look. What you offer. You must accept and love everything that makes up the person that is you. You see, the first step on the LovePath is *attraction*. If you believe you are unattractive, that will affect how others see you as well. You have to believe in you."

Sounds Pollyannaish, doesn't it? Like pop psychology you can read in any magazine off the grocery store shelf, all with little application in real life. Nevertheless, it is the absolute truth. To *be* attractive, you must first *believe* you are so, and then you must work on all the areas where you believe you are not.

My job with Lisa was to help her understand that falling in love is a process. When people follow that process in the right way, they fall in love, whether they mean to or not. When they vacate or violate that process, they fall out of love, whether they mean to or not.

I showed Lisa the LovePath—all of it. That was many years ago. I also was at her wedding a couple years after that. Today she is happily married. Her sons have two fathers and the stepfather gives himself to them as fully as any biological dad ever has. This is the power—and the joy—of leading people on the LovePath.

As Lisa discovered, the first step on the LovePath is critical. And it all depends on you.

You can do it. I will show you how.

## THE PATH OF LIFE

There are several important reasons why we speak of the love experience as a path. One is that the idea of a path helps us understand that love is a process. It is not an isolated event. If we understand the beginning and end of the process, as well as the twists and turns that come along the path, then we will be better travelers. Would you take an important business trip or vacation to a place you've never been before without studying a map? If you didn't use a map or GPS, you might get to your destination eventually, but only after many wrong turns and some unhappy circumstances.

Let this book be your road map for a life of love. Let it guide you on your journey to learn the art of falling—and staying—in love.

The second reason we speak of a path is that it shows us where to walk tomorrow. It gives us hope and the chance for a new beginning. If you have never been in love, isn't it wonderful to know the lay of the land before you pass through? And if you have been in love, whether you're single, married, or single again, knowing the path will help you understand where you've been, how you got off the path (if that happened), and how you can get back on track again.

Perhaps the most exciting truth about the LovePath is that it shows the way toward falling in love. Or falling in love all over again.

If you've been in a bad relationship, it's understandable that you find it impossible to turn the bad to good. There are situations, particularly those involving abuse, which must be left behind. But in other cases, miracles still occur. People simply come to a clearer understanding of themselves, their spouses, and their love relationships—and everything changes. It's like standing atop a hill so that they can see, from above, the path they've walked from attraction to acceptance to attachment to aspiration (the basic components of the LovePath). They can understand where they left the path and got lost. In addition, they can see the way to begin the attraction process again and walk together in a deeper, more fulfilling relationship.

Let us climb that imaginary hill and look outward, so that we can take in the entire path. For now, we will not go into detail. We will look at the overall map so that we know where we are going. And as we do that, you will begin to think about the pathway you've already walked. You may even find yourself thinking, "Of course! I've been there."

When that happens, you'll want to "zoom in," as you might do with a map on the Internet, and get the fine details. Well, don't worry. We promise to "zoom in" on each stage of the journey. At the proper time.

For now, let's discover how the path is laid.

## THE BIG PICTURE

The LovePath is my personal name for a well-charted journey. There are different views about the specifics of the path. For example, some researchers suggest that the motivations that bring two humans together are lust, attraction, and attachment.

My own view is that the LovePath consists of the following:

- Attraction
- Acceptance
- Attachment
- Aspiration

The following illustration shows the process.

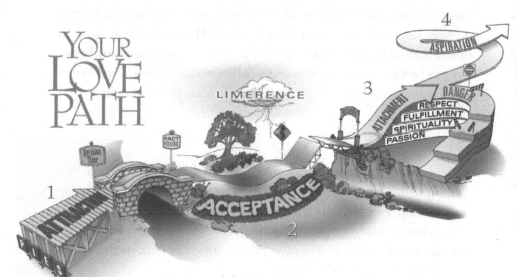

## Attraction

Very simply, our relationships generally begin with *attraction*. As we will discover in the next few pages, there are many interesting factors that help determine the person to whom we are attracted, and why.

When we look for a permanent, fulfilling relationship, we seek someone who attracts us physically, mentally, emotionally, and spiritually. *Attraction* is about the process of deciding to draw closer.

## Acceptance

This is the stage of determining whether we can indeed share who we really are with this potential mate. This portion of the path is all about honesty, openness, and vulnerability. In the previous stage, we were attracted to what might be described as the "picture" of someone—who they appear to be and who we hope they are. We all try to project the best personal image that we can to others, and we do this to an even greater extent when we are looking for love. However, is it an accurate warts-and-all image? At the point of acceptance, we learn how honest we can be with another person and whether we'll still be accepted when we tell our secrets and reveal our flaws. Acceptance is about caring.

## Attachment

This stage is about commitment. When we feel truly accepted by a person to whom we are attracted, there's a strong likelihood that the relationship will evolve to the point of attaching ourselves together in a committed relationship. The most obvious form of this is the legal attachment of marriage. However, there are other important levels of connection that we need to experience.

First, there is the sense of fulfillment, which everyone craves. Second, there should be mutual respect. Third, passion for each other must endure. Fourth, there should be a truly spiritual adventure shared between the two people. A much longer time is involved in the attachment stage, so there is more time for things to go wrong. However, even in the midst of our mistakes, there are many steps we can take to reconnect with each other and build a deeper love.

## Aspiration

This final stage is where a relationship passes from the ordinary to the extraordinary. Each of us grew up with ideas of what we wanted to be, what our families or marriages would be like, and what we would accomplish. These aspirations may be conscious or subconscious. We may be able to articulate them to another, or we may not discover we have them until we reach a point where we expected them and they did not occur.

According to Dr. John Gottman at the University of Washington's Love Lab, these dreams usually come from childhood and are either something we want to re-create or something we want to avoid.

Because these aspirations are sometimes subconscious, couples seldom share them with each other before they commit to marriage. Even when they are conscious, an amazing number of couples still do not talk about them, each simply *expecting* or *assuming* the other has or supports the same aspirations. More often, couples' unspoken dreams compete, which means either one or both cannot achieve his or her dreams.

In a marriage that grows—I like to think of it as continually spiraling upward—each person works to help the other reach his or her aspirations, even when they seem contradictory to one's own. That can be accomplished through compromise, which will be discussed in a later chapter. However, the majority of marriages do not spiral upward. They either stagnate in a stalemate of bitterness or resigned acceptance, or they spiral downward to their own destruction.

The key word in a marriage that spirals upward is *cooperation*. The key word in a marriage that spirals downward to destruction is *control*. One spouse dominates the other, getting his or her way, and stifling any hope the other has of achieving his or her dreams. When I see a relationship like that, it reminds me there is one thing true of all dictators: someone wants them to disappear.

I am sure many questions come to mind as you think about these components. You might want to know exactly what we mean by passion or what constitutes fulfillment. You might think it's impossible to experience all these things in a long-term relationship. But don't worry.

*The key word in a marriage that spirals upward is* cooperation. *The key word in a marriage that spirals downward to destruction is* control.

It's not impossible. And we will explain.

For now, however, let's begin with the first step of the journey.

## UNDERSTANDING ATTRACTION

Life is made of moments—thousands, even millions, of individual moments. Some are wonderful, some unbearable. The vast majority are, well, just plain old moments.

We all have our defining moments. These are those remarkable instances in time when our lives change forever. We never forget them. Getting your driver's license may have been a defining moment for you. What about your first date? Maybe a religious experience?

Then there is that day when you meet the special man or woman whom you eventually choose as a partner for life. If you are now or have ever been married, you can probably describe in vivid detail how and when the two of you first met. If I were there to see your face as you told the story, I would likely see your eyes shine and a smile appear.

Something attracted at least one of you to the other; eventually there had to be a mutual attraction, or no attachment would result. How exactly does that work? How does one person out of thousands make such an impression upon us?

Attraction is a powerful force, one many researchers have tried to explain. A great deal of study has been devoted to the question of why and how people divide themselves two by two. But, as we all know, there is no simple answer.

Several different factors come into play.

We know that physical, intellectual, emotional, and spiritual matters all play a part in attraction. If a person is attractive in only one of these areas, we may be drawn to him or her. If that person has two, three, or all four of the dimensions of attraction, the draw is that much stronger.

Let us look at each of these.

## Physical Attraction (Body)

What would you expect to be the first point of attraction? The most obvious answer is appearance. After all, you cannot love someone for his or her mind if you do not know that mind yet. You cannot feel an emotional bonding with someone you have not met.

However, you *can* like what you see.

It's a fact: attractive people catch our eye. What are the physical elements you look for? The answer can be depicted fairly simply in a picture. The first time we meet someone, the only data we have on him or her is the physical. That's the simplest "picture" we have of them. We all know that you cannot judge a book by its cover, but in a bookstore, it *is* the cover that causes us to pick up the book and find out a little more about it.

Studies of people in various cultures, all across the world, show that men, consciously or subconsciously, tend to be attracted to the physical features, especially those that demonstrate health and the ability to bear children. Why do men care about nice teeth and shiny hair? These are basic indicators of health. Why do men look at hips and breasts in women? Because they relate to childbirth. Do all men know that's what appeals to them? No. But research suggests that the most desirable ratio of a woman's waist to hips, in the eyes of a man, is 70 to 80 percent, which turns out to be the ideal dimension for bearing children.

The same studies tell a different story for women. What are they looking for in a man? When looking for short-term relationships, the physical tends to carry more significance, but when looking for long-term relationships other factors of attraction tend to matter more.

*Quit worrying that all the gorgeous people will take all the good ones out there. . . . There is a lot more to attraction than physical attraction.*

What physical attributes tend to attract women?

Is he tall? Does he have a flat stomach? Muscles and broad shoulders? It can be described in one word: *dominance.* (Notice that this is not domination. Most people are repulsed by the idea of being dominated by another.) When we refer to dominance, we do so in the context of physical prowess, emotional strength, social position, wealth, ability to succeed in life, or any other factor—or combination of factors—that indicates that a man can father healthy children and provide for their safety and their future. Women tend to want someone strong enough to establish a home and protect a wife and children, even if they do not intend to be homemakers. One important area of their assessment is the physical makeup of a man.

However, physical appearance is not a first-look-only issue. Our looks continue to be a factor in maintaining attractiveness. As time goes on, though we lose our youthful appeal, the physical aspect of attraction is always there, always a consideration.

Does that mean those who are not physically attractive by Madison Avenue standards will not find true love? Absolutely not. Physical attraction is only one of the four areas of attraction. Those of us who wish that God had done a little more sculpting on our physical features will discover that we have as much opportunity for romance and life-long love as the "beautiful" people. How? By being attractive in one or more of the remaining three aspects of attraction. It may seem like common sense—and there is research to back it up—but the more deeply you fall in love with another person, the more physically attractive you tend to find that person to be.

So be as physically attractive as you can be at your age and situation in life. Take care of your body. Wash your hair and brush your teeth. Eat right and exercise. Dress well and walk with confidence. Quit worrying that all the gorgeous people will take all the good ones out there. As we will see, there is a lot more to attraction than physical attraction.

## Intellectual Attraction (Mind)

Deepest love requires us to make a connection with body, mind, heart, and soul. Have you ever been powerfully attracted to someone with fashion-model looks, a "perfect ten," then realized the person who lives in that beautiful body isn't attractive at all? How about the other way around? Ever met an individual who didn't strike you as particularly attractive at first, but over time, as you got to know that person, he or she began to look better to you?

Intellectual attraction (mind) occurs when someone stimulates your thinking. You realize that this is a person with whom you can have meaningful conversations, someone with whom you are proud to be associated, and who stimulates you to grow mentally.

Consider this scenario. A woman meets a handsome athlete to whom she is immediately physically attracted. Because of the "halo effect"—which leads us to believe that if a person has an obvious positive attribute, such as physical attractiveness, that person has *all* positive attributes—she will likely assume that he is intelligent, kind, loving, and has all sorts of other attributes that she wants in a man. But over time, she realizes he has absolutely no awareness of the current events and issues about which she is passionate. He is an extreme sports enthusiast while she cares nothing for sports. They have little to nothing in common other than their physical desire for each other. Could they connect? Absolutely. People may be drawn closer by any of the four aspects of attraction. However, it is much more likely that they will not connect if she is interested in a long-term relationship. Pretty bodies are exciting, without doubt, but physical beauty and prowess are fleeting at best. In a few years, she would be much happier with a man who has a beautiful mind rather than one with a fading body.

As a general rule, pretty people—male or female—have the edge when someone seeks a short-term relationship. But unless they are also intellectually, emotionally, and spiritually attractive, the relationship tends to turn sour with time. Similarly, people who are not immediately seen as physically attractive may initially be rejected because of the halo effect (if we think one attribute is undesirable, we tend to believe that all attributes are undesirable). However, when the person who initially passed them by gets to know and understand their intellectual, emotional, and spiritual attractiveness, the rejected become desirable.

Because of the halo effect, they may even become more physically attractive! Take heart if you are not in the category of "swimsuit model" or "Hollywood hunk." If you are a person with a good mind, a wonderful heart, and spiritual depth, you actually have a definite advantage when someone is looking for a long-term relationship. Therefore, be as physically attractive as you can at your age and situation in life for your own self-esteem, but disabuse yourself of the idea that you will only be attractive through plastic surgery. Put that effort into developing your mind, heart, and soul.

It pays off far better.

Intellectual attraction is important whether we consider ourselves intellectual or not. We tend to want relationships with people who stimulate us and challenge us, rather than dulling us. Keep growing your mind, and you will be ever attractive to yourself and others.

## Emotional Attraction (Heart)

We first look upon the visual package, then we probe the mind, and then we want to know what lies in the heart. As you noticed, we start with the most easily discovered level of attraction and then gradually move deeper into what makes a person who he or she is.

*Emotions decide more of our actions than we generally care to recognize.*

Yes, body and brain are primary considerations. However, there is more to being a couple than good looks, reading similar books, and voting the same political ticket. People also want to know that they are a good fit on the emotional level.

Feelings usually outweigh facts. Emotions decide more of our actions than we generally care to recognize.

What are we looking for in the emotional realm? It ranges from laughter to security to feeling truly understood. In general we want a relationship with a person who makes us feel the way we wish to feel, who evokes emotions within us that we enjoy.

It may be someone who makes us enjoy ourselves.

"What do you see in him?" asks one young lady of another.

"He makes me laugh," she responds.

A sense of humor indicates both intelligence and feeling. Humor bonds people by breaking down barriers between them. Once we laugh together, we feel closer. We identify more personally. We may view a humorless individual—often incorrectly, by the way—as less likely to be sensitive and feeling. But many of us value a sense of humor because of what it implies about a person, that they're caring and feeling. We're not necessarily looking for the tiresome class clown, but rather for someone who makes us laugh and feel good about life.

We also tend to want to bond with a person who makes us feel safe and secure, someone who will protect us from any enemy, real or imagined. We want to know that he or she is "with me no matter what," and will never abandon or leave us alone, frightened with nowhere to turn.

We also want a person who understands us. So much of life is about how we *feel*. It is important, then, to find someone who cares about our emotions.

Connecting emotionally is a very important step in this stage, just as it will continue to be a crucial factor throughout the life of the relationship. Emotional attraction is finally established when both people display caring, tenderness, and emotional investment in each other.

When is emotional attraction unimportant to people? Typically, when they don't care if a relationship lasts, don't care about other people as much as they do themselves, or don't care about themselves at all. Short-term specialists want a partner with the best body, someone who will make others envy them. Their concern is not for the other but for themselves. "Use them and lose them" is the motto by which they live. They do not care for emotional connection because they do not want to *give* emotional connection.

Take my advice: if you wish to master the art of falling in love, run from short-term specialists and wait for the long-term relationship that is out there seeking you. If you invest time in the temporary satisfaction of the short-term, you will miss the long-term when it presents itself to you. As they saying goes, forget about Mr. Right Now and focus on finding Mr. Right (or Miss Right, as the case may be).

## Spiritual Attraction (Soul)

Finally, there is the understanding of the human soul. With this stage, we go as deep as one can, from the simple picture to the genuine and authentic person who has attracted our attention.

How is this spiritual element different from the emotional one? We want someone to understand us, but we also want someone to inspire us. Most of us are in search of someone who makes us feel, "I want to be like you on the inside, and I want my children to be like you."

Personal beliefs and values come into play here. People tend to look for companions who share their view of right and wrong, of what is important in life, and the guidelines by which life should be lived.

Sometimes just finding a person with similar spirituality—similar beliefs and values—is enough for a relationship to get started and grow to fruition. In a world gone topsy-turvy, shared values and beliefs are becoming more important in determining long-term attraction.

Therefore, people often seek mates within their own religion, though we also see many blends of faith. Unfortunately, some couples fall in love and ignore this spiritual component of the relationship, believing it is personal and private rather than a relationship dynamic. Then comes the birth of children—and this element flies to the forefront. If a Baptist and a Catholic marry, for example (or a couple from Jewish and Christian beliefs), how will the children be taught about religion? Certainly that question needs to be worked out sooner rather than later. Great conflicts can occur if serious discussions about faith are neglected until children are conceived.

*In a world gone topsy-turvy, shared values and beliefs are becoming more important in determining long-term attraction.*

Your personal spirituality may range anywhere from fundamentalism to atheism. Whatever your beliefs may be, do not overlook the spiritual element of attraction. Even the secular researchers are writing that for a marriage relationship to reach its highest levels of fulfillment, there must be a shared spiritual component. That means shared meaning for life, purpose, values, morals, and deep beliefs. Ignore this dimension of attraction and it will come back to bite you later. Your spiritual beliefs make you who you are and guide you through life. You would be wise to make sure that any person you seek relationship with has compatible beliefs. Otherwise, trouble lies on the horizon.

## LOVE AND ATTRACTION

Physical, intellectual, emotional, and spiritual attraction all play a part in the beginning of love, because they are all a part of who we are. (You can remember these four kinds of attraction with the acronym PIES.)

The visible, physical element usually comes first, unless perhaps you meet your mate in an Internet chat room. It makes sense that we proceed logically through getting to know the mind, the heart, and finally the soul. However, these aspects are not self-dependent stages of attraction. They all work in cooperation. They will continue to determine the increasing or decreasing level of attraction between two people over a lifetime. It is as much an ongoing process after fifty years of marriage as it is after fifty minutes of becoming acquainted.

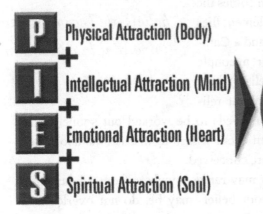

Attraction is not a section of the path that we leave forever, even after moving on to the next stage. It is a continuing dynamic. Those who find fulfillment in love are those who continue to be attracted to each other.

It is also true that there is no perfect combination of body, mind, heart, and soul. The balance of the facets of attraction is a little different for every relationship. If there were such a thing as perfect love, we would excel in every area: the two would truly become one, almost inseparable as individuals. However, people are complex. Some are better developed intellectually than emotionally. Some will never be doctoral candidates at the university, but they have wonderful, caring hearts. Others are superb spiritual leaders who help us grow in that arena.

We all have a different "mix," but we do not want to be deficient in any area that determines who we are and how we connect with someone else.

To make yourself the most attractive you can possibly be, take care of your body, stimulate your mind, find peace and happiness in your heart, and provide for your soul. You may eventually choose a companion who is not attractive in all four areas, if one or more areas are powerful enough in attracting you, but all these dimensions are important.

If you are single, pay attention to all four areas as you analyze whether first meetings move to first dates that continue to second dates. If you are married, do all you can to develop yourself in each of these areas. Do it for your spouse, but most important, do it for yourself. It feels good and gives great confidence to know that you are as attractive as you can be at your age and situation in life, rather than having some lonely pity party, lamenting how others may be more attractive than you.

And never forget to believe in yourself! The more attractive you believe you are—not just physically, but in all four areas—the more your confidence makes you attractive.

Remember Lisa? The woman whose husband abandoned her? That is what I helped her understand about herself. As long as she saw herself as too old to compete with the twenty-somethings, she would be. If she viewed having children as a negative to most men she would meet, her own unconscious actions might make that so. If she continued to believe that no good men were out there, for her there would not be.

James Allen, British philosopher, wrote the following in the classic *As a Man Thinketh*:

"As a man thinketh in his heart so is he," embraces the whole of a man's being. A man is literally what he thinks, his character being the complete sum of all his thoughts. As the plant springs from, and could not be without, the seed, so every act of a man springs from the hidden seeds of thought, and could not have appeared without them. This applies equally to those acts called "spontaneous" and "unpremeditated" as to those which are deliberately executed. . . .

Of all the beautiful truths pertaining to the soul which have been restored and brought to light in this age, none is more gladdening or fruitful of divine promise and confidence than this—that man is the master of thought, the molder of character, and maker and shaper of condition, environment, and destiny. . . .

The soul attracts that which it secretly harbors; that which it loves, and also that which it fears. It reaches the height of its cherished aspirations. . . .

Every thought seed sown or allowed to fall into the mind, and to take root there, produces its own, blossoming sooner or later into act, and bearing its own fruitage of opportunity and circumstance. Good thoughts bear good fruit, bad thoughts bad fruit.

I told Lisa about a woman who walked into a seminar that I conducted a few years ago. I am quite sure if we had calculated her Body Mass Index, it would have indicated she was obese. However, I have never seen a woman walk into a room with more belief in her own beauty and sexuality. She dressed the part and carried the air of a star. Interestingly, every man in that room turned to watch her—and kept their eyes on her until well after she took her seat. Later my helper in the seminar commented on how attractive she was. She demonstrated as clearly as I have ever seen this powerful truth: you are as attractive as you believe you are.

Lisa stopped thinking of her age as a limitation but rather as an asset. She refused to think of her being a mother as a potential negative to suitors but instead as an indication of her stability, responsibility, and ability to love. She began to exercise, to dress well, to care for her body and looks. She enrolled in continuing education classes, made time to be with friends and socialize, and became very active in her church. In short she worked on her own physical, mental, emotional, and spiritual well-being. And she did it for herself, not for some man who might exist in her future. As a result, she found inner happiness that led to her being attractive to the point that many men sought her attention. From those she finally chose one to develop a relationship with and marry.

We want to be physically, intellectually, emotionally, and spiritually attractive people, first for ourselves, and then for the partner we have (or may one day have).

## YOUR ATTRACTIVENESS

How does an attraction-mix work between people? Let us think about the balance of the four kinds of attraction we have discussed. Imagine for a moment what happens when relationships are dominated significantly by one component. The effect could be something like this:

- Mostly physical attraction: a sexual relationship
- Mostly intellectual attraction: a challenging companionship
- Mostly emotional attraction: a warm friendship
- Mostly spiritual attraction: a contemplative partnership

Most relationships, of course, have a more complex mixture of the four components. Many of them begin with physical attraction, but in time they grow in the other areas.

On the other hand, one factor may be almost completely absent. There are relationships devoid of physical attraction, for example, or lacking in the sharing of intellect. In some relationships there is no true spiritual component. A relationship without one or more of the dimensions will likely never be as close, wonderful, and fulfilling as it could have been if that aspect were present.

Think about yourself, as others are likely to know you. If your friends were asked to describe you to a stranger, what adjectives would they use? If they were asked to enumerate your strengths, what would they list first? Go ahead and write down a few key words.

Next, while you have paper and pencil handy, draw four lines—one for each kind of attractiveness: physical, intellectual, emotional, and spiritual. Now think about yourself on a scale from 1 to 7:

> 1 = extremely unattractive
> 2 = very unattractive
> 3 = somewhat unattractive
> 4 = mixed
> 5 = somewhat attractive
> 6 = very attractive
> 7 = extremely attractive

On each PIES factor (physical, intellectual, emotional, and spiritual), rate your level of attractiveness. Remember, we are not comparing ourselves with absolute ideals—supermodels in the physical category or Mother Teresa in the spiritual one. We are talking about average folks you meet on the street or see in church.

*If your friends were asked to describe you to a stranger, what adjectives would they use?*

What surprises you about your results? Where do you have the highest rating? Where is there most room for improvement?

Draw four more lines. This time, measure where you would *like* to be and the levels you could realistically attain. For example, on your physical attractiveness graph, the idea of becoming a 7 may be unrealistic if you honestly estimate yourself to be a 1 at present. On the other hand, perhaps you rated yourself a 1 because you are obese and with proper diet and exercise, you *could* become a 7. Determine what you can actually accomplish. Set attainable goals.

You will find that in each area, there are practical steps you can take to make yourself more attractive. As you consider each category, list some of these steps. Most of us feel that we could do more with our physical appearance, which is that first impression we make. Can you join the local health club? Do something new with your hair? Go to an upscale store and ask a specialist to help you choose a new wardrobe, even if you can afford to buy only one piece at a time?

If you feel the need to become more intellectually attractive, you could join a book club. Find an area of learning that really stimulates you, and perhaps take some evening courses at a local college or find a course online.

If you want to be emotionally more attractive, think about the feelings you have and how they come into play with your relationships. Do you have a healthy self-love? Do you tend to be emotionally possessive or emotionally distant? Maybe you need to see a counselor or pastor to help you with your emotions. You may even need a physician to write you a prescription for anxiety or depression.

If you wish to be spiritually more attractive, you must look within to find what you believe, value, and cherish. If you have been religious but have slacked in your involvement, start over. Learn to meditate, pray, and give of yourself to others. This may be the right time to make an appointment with a religious leader in whom you can have confidence, and ask for guidance to help you grow spiritually. The idea is to be proactive. Do not lie around feeling sorry for yourself. Take positive steps to grow, to be what you want to be.

We realize personal growth, change, and improvement can be challenging. We cannot easily change who we are, but we can grow to a new level. You might need some help and advice, but you are on the right track!

## BECOMING MORE ATTRACTIVE

Where does all this rating and writing leave you? If you created your own attractiveness profile, you should have some good indications of what factors make you attractive. Congratulations! Every one of us has something beautiful and compelling about us. You might have been reminded that you are a person of warmth and compassion, or that you have a quick and incisive mind. It might be that you are devout in your spiritual beliefs and, as such, you were made to bless someone else with your depth of wisdom.

You will also have created a picture of where there is room for growth. The wonderful truth is that in each of the four categories, there is something we can do to make ourselves more attractive. Isn't it exciting to know that we can not only make ourselves more attractive to others but also find a deeper self-satisfaction as we nurture our own growth?

As we began talking about the LovePath, we discussed the fact that it is a path we can choose to travel, and one to which we can return after losing our way. Since attraction comes at the beginning of the journey, we can always come back to it. It is never too late to become a more pleasant, impressive, and magnetic person who is physically dynamic, intellectually compelling, emotionally accessible, and spiritually profound.

Such a person will love and be loved on the path to a life of fulfillment.

## CHAPTER SUMMARY

*The art of falling in love is a path or process. It has four steps:*
- Attraction—we draw closer to a person we find attractive.
- Acceptance—we grow to care for a person whom we accept as he or she is, and who accepts us as we truly are.
- Attachment—when we come to care enough for a person, we commit ourselves to a relationship with that person.
- Aspiration—to reach the deepest level of love, we cooperate with our lover so that each of us may attain his or her dreams and life desires.

*We are attracted to people because of any of four areas, but strongest attraction comes from a combination of the four:*
- Physical—we are drawn to someone whose body we find attractive.
- Intellectual—we are drawn to people who stimulate and interest our minds.
- Emotional—we are drawn to people who generate positive emotions within us.

• Spiritual—we are drawn to people who inspire us or who share our beliefs and values.

By believing in and properly loving oneself, anyone can become more attractive in each of these four areas. When we do that for ourselves first, we are, in turn, more attractive to others.

Attraction remains important throughout the life of a relationship.

# STEP TWO:
# ACCEPTANCE

# THE CRAVING
# FOR CARING

*You cannot genuinely* love someone if you do not accept him or her for who he or she is—even if that someone is you.

Grab a pen or a highlighter and go back to the paragraph just above. Mark that sentence. Memorize it. This bedrock truth about relationships is *essential* to understand.

Allow me to make it clearer. True love means accepting a person as he or she truly is. If you put any conditions on a person for them to receive your love, it is *not* that person you love; it is the picture you want that person to paint for you. Your love exists as long as they pretend to be what you wish, and fades if they cease to be the imaginary person into which you have made them.

Also, did you catch that this is just as true of your love for yourself? If you cannot accept yourself as you are—if you put criteria on yourself that you must meet to feel loveable—then you do *not* love *you* in a healthy way. That doesn't preclude growing and becoming better. Rather, it means that *healthy* self-love is being able to accept who you are now rather than who you were in the past or will be in the future. It means loving yourself as you are rather than loving a picture you paint for anyone.

Including you.

Now let me give you another bedrock truth that is just as powerful: accepting another as he or she truly is has the power to lead him or her to fall in love with you.

## HIDING BEHIND THE WALL

As children, we learned how painful rejection is. We also learned that a guaranteed way to avoid rejection—at least on the surface—is to pretend to be what we think someone else wants us to be. We learned to build a metaphorical wall behind which we hide, and on the other side of the wall—the side that others see—we paint whatever picture is needed to gain acceptance. We may change the picture based on the situation or people from whom we crave acceptance, or from whom we fear rejection. That is why many people tend to be different at work, at home, at church, at social events, and more. They have different environments, different people, different pictures to fit into and be accepted. The problem is that none of those pictures is a true image of the real person.

Perhaps you seldom let one or both parents see who you really were because whenever they perceived you were not as they wished you to be, they hurt you. It may not have been a physical hurt, but emotional, mental, and spiritual hurt can be just as devastating and just as scarring, even if others cannot readily see those scars. Criticism, contempt, and emotional abandonment can be powerful weapons to coerce behavior or thinking.

Therefore, we learn how to dress to gain acceptance from the folks with whom we wish to fit in, how to talk their language, how to mimic their ideas or beliefs, and how to act.

However, each of us desires—*deeply* desires—to be loved for the person we really are behind our wall, rather than the pictures we paint on it. We crave the opportunity for total honesty and transparency without fear of ridicule or rejection. We long for someone to know the good, the bad, *and* the ugly, and to love us anyway. We want to have our souls go naked, without shame or reservation, with the inner peace that we do not have to pretend to feel lovely and loveable. Unfortunately, many never develop a relationship like that, even if they marry, but the longing never goes away.

How does one find it? How does one find the courage to be that transparent? It comes in an environment of acceptance. Accepting self. Being accepted by another.

That is the core of love.

## A PICTURE OR YOU?

The picture on a person's wall is often what first attracts someone. As we said in the last chapter, attraction is most often about physical appearance, but we could also be attracted to the mind, heart, or soul of another person without even seeing him. It could happen through a series of e-mails, an acquaintance struck up through an Internet chat room, or even a voice we have heard on the telephone while dealing with an out-of-town client at work. We are drawn to someone in body, mind, heart, soul, or usually some combination of the four.

But here's the thing. When we're attracted to that picture, most of us never stop to think, "Is it the real person attracting me or is it my perception of that person?" Or, "Is this person attracted to me, or to a picture I have painted?"

That picture may or may not be an accurate representation. King Henry VIII of England had six wives during his lifetime. The fourth, Anne of Cleves, received a marriage proposal based on her beautiful portrait, painted by the finest German painter. When the king met his fiancée, he was appalled at the difference between the person and the picture. The two were divorced within a year.

Images can be deceiving, can't they? Most of the time, however, the process of learning the difference between an image and the "real thing" is not as simple as it was for the king of England. The pictures we see are not painted on canvas. Rather, our picture of someone is based on a composite of perceptions we have gathered. It is the sum of all the positive qualities the person has carefully projected, minus the negative qualities that are just as carefully hidden. Add to that the subjective nature of our own observations and our willingness to see what we want to see in people . . . well, it all combines to form the halo effect, where, if we like one thing about a person, we project that attitude toward everything else about the person.

This is not as false or hypocritical as it sounds. How cynical would love be if we greeted any new acquaintance with deep suspicion, distrust, and cold-hearted realism? We choose to be people of hope. It is healthy and right to see the best in others, as well as to project the best in ourselves. There will be plenty of time for establishing transparency later.

We move on, then, toward building a relationship. We begin dating—an activity that seems to be about dinner or a movie, but is really a kind of research trip or fact-finding mission. Through a series of dates, we begin to move closer to the truth. For example, simple observation will indicate that our date is not perfect after all. We see with our own eyes that our date becomes angry in traffic, or is sloppy or cheap.

*The more time we spend together, the more we long to be honest and share who we really are.*

The more time we spend together, the more difficult it is for us to imitate perfection—and the more we long to be honest and share who we really are. As we draw closer to sharing our genuine selves, and as we stay connected despite our imperfections, we move into the *acceptance* phase. *Attraction* is about moving closer, and *acceptance* is about caring for the authentic human being we find behind the picture.

This crucial phase of the relationship establishes the honesty that will become the relationship's foundation—or the dishonesty that will eventually be its downfall. We know that in today's world, such honesty can prove difficult to find, sometimes even when two people are on their way to the church to be married.

Do these problems arise because someone has intentionally lied or withheld the truth? Not at all. Quite often, problems arise because of what we *think* was communicated or promised, only to find it hasn't come true.

Let's explore an example through the story of Bill and Yvonne.

## BILL AND YVONNE

The first thing Yvonne noticed about Bill was his shiny red sports car. Sure, she knew it was superficial, but that was the truth. Bill's Porsche convertible made quite an impression. Then, once the two began to chat, Yvonne found out that Bill himself was not so bad, even away from his car.

For Bill, it was Yvonne's long, blond hair, then her fun-loving personality. She was everything he had dreamed about in a girlfriend. The two of them were immediately attracted to each other, and a one-year courtship led to marriage.

While they were dating, Bill would take Yvonne on long, Sunday-afternoon drives in the convertible with the top down. He loved seeing the wind blow her hair as they cruised along mountain roads. After the wedding, the couple loved taking spontaneous weekend trips at a moment's notice, driving along the coast until they found an inviting inn somewhere near the beach. They talked about their dreams occasionally: Bill wanted to upgrade to a newer and more powerful Porsche and then travel across America in it. Yvonne could imagine a roomful of children.

Five years passed, and Yvonne began to feel uncomfortable. They were childless; Bill never thought the timing was right. She began to raise the subject more frequently and more urgently; Bill became irritable. He wanted to know why Yvonne was starting to nag so much. That was not something she used to do at all.

The tension began to spread into other issues. One day Yvonne could not seem to get Bill's attention while he was searching for some item in his back issues of *Car and Driver* magazine.

"Are sports cars all you ever think about?"

Bill looked up. "What are you talking about? You knew my hobby from the first moment we met. I thought my Porsche was what made an impression on you."

"It was," she replied. "But it wasn't the reason I fell in love with you."

"Well, what exactly did you expect?"

"I expected you to grow up. Sure, the car was cool. I always got a kick out of it. But I expected you to become a husband eventually, and yes, even a father."

Bill rolled his eyes. "Children again. I knew exactly where this was going."

"Bill, we've been married five years. We only have a window of time while we're young for starting a family, and . . ."

"Last time I checked, there's no law requiring us to start one."

"How can you *do* that?" Yvonne was nearly shouting now. "How can you pretend we didn't agree to have children?"

"What on earth are you talking about? I never promised to start a family."

"Don't you remember all those road trips? How I would talk about boys and girls and the family names . . ."

"That's what you wanted to talk about. Did you ever once hear me say I wanted that, too? On the other hand, I do recall talking about saving for a new Porsche, which you will not let me do. I can't keep a penny that you haven't set aside for some new piece of furniture."

"We need a nice home!"

"Who says? Where is that written? I always said I wanted to pack a toothbrush, two changes of clothing, sell everything else, and drive across America. How many times did I tell you that was my dream?"

"I knew it was your dream, but we were stupid kids. Real adults outgrow that stuff. How realistic is it to plan on living in your car? How can you raise children without a house or a home?"

"Exactly. Which is the whole point of not having children."

Yvonne sat and stared at her husband for a moment before

responding. "I don't know you. I don't know who I married. I thought you were being honest. I thought you were serious about the future, about your faith, for that matter. You went to church with me every weekend until we got married."

Bill realized their disagreement was moving to a new and dangerous level and he made a renewed attempt to control his simmering anger. "I went to church because it was somewhere you wanted to go. I figured it was a nice thing to do for you, okay? I had no idea I was committing myself to packing a lousy pew every single Sunday for the rest of my life! Yvonne, you know I don't like living my life confined, whether in a sanctuary or in some decorator home. It makes me crazy!"

"I know that." Yvonne's tears began. "I know that, but I thought you saw the same future I saw. I thought getting married was all about building a family. I thought we were agreeing on those things when we decided to get married."

"We never talked about any of it," Bill said. "I thought getting married was all about continuing to do what you already enjoyed, only with the one person you've chosen. I thought you knew who I was and what I enjoyed."

With that, the conversation—and, in Bill's and Yvonne's minds, their marriage—ended.

## What Did You Expect?

With whom did you identify in that story? Who is in the right, and who is in the wrong?

The truth is that this story has no hero and no villain. These are simply two young lovers who understood two different plans for their relationship. They were pushing in different directions.

It happens all the time. We desire a particular person and a particular future. We want both of them so much that we make ourselves believe the person and the purpose will somehow interlock. Somewhere in the early excitement of falling in love, we lose sight of the details that will become vital down the road. Remember, during the attraction phase, we are drawn to the picture, not the person. During the acceptance phase, we need to be very clear about what and whom we really accept.

Think about this question: What if Bill and Yvonne had done a better job of not only sharing their dreams but also establishing what each wanted from life and marriage? Wouldn't that have caused the same problem, but up front? Would the conflicting dreams constitute a deal-breaker in their engagement? Bill *did* talk about the trip across America; Yvonne *did* verbalize her love of children. But what if the couple had sat down together and spelled out their goals, and taken each other's dreams very seriously? Would they have come to the understanding that marriage between them was not going to work out?

*Somewhere in the early excitement of falling in love, we lose sight of the details that will become vital down the road.*

Not necessarily.

Conflicting goals must be met head on, but there are often strategies for working them out. In a later chapter, we will revisit Bill and Yvonne and discover how they worked together to help each other pursue their dreams as a happily married couple pushing forward in a united direction.

It is a healthy exercise for any couple to talk about expectations as clearly—and as early—as possible. If you did not do so before you were married, or if you did not do so as thoroughly as you could have, it is never too late. What are your thoughts on where a relationship should lead? What kind of family have you dreamed about having, and why? Where do you see yourself living five years from now, and if you have a career, where is that heading?

As a couple, make your separate lists and then compare them. Discuss them and look together for ways to help each other move toward his or her dreams. Be creative about finding ways to fit those dreams together as one.

If you are single and not a part of a romantic relationship, it is still important to know exactly who you are and what your goals for the future may be. Have you ever put them on paper? Have you created a mission statement for your life? If not, give it a try! Ask yourself the questions in the preceding paragraph. Then, at some point in the future, as you grow serious in a love relationship, encourage your partner to do the same thing. If he or she attempts to change who you are, seriously consider moving on. That *will not* get better if you were to marry.

Can you see how wise and how productive such an exercise would be for two individuals who love one another? Can you imagine how many future arguments, and how much tension and misery, could be avoided?

I encourage you to take a sheet of paper and write, "What do I expect?" at the top. Making that list may help you learn more about yourself than anything else you have ever done. It may free you to focus on the things that matter most to you in life.

## Deeper into Acceptance

Let us return for a moment to the idea of what happens as you draw closer to someone and begin to care. On that first date, your discussions center on safe topics. You are likely to talk about the music and the movies that the two of you like, as well as what you enjoy doing in your free time. If you have a career, that subject is likely to come up. You might even touch on your career goals, as long as there is nothing too controversial about them.

We deepen our relationship by sharing facts that define who we are.

Which facts? At first, the most inoffensive and ordinary ones. Whenever we meet new people, we exchange names and tell "what we do": primary information that requires no real transparency. The more we talk and the longer we spend getting to know each other, the more personal the facts we share. In time, if we are honest with each other, we will discuss past mistakes, matters of personal history, and even subjects that require a painful level of honesty.

We also begin to move from facts to feelings. Our emotions, of course, say much more about who we are than do the facts of our lives. All of us have deep-rooted feelings about things from politics to morality, from spirituality to sexuality and the nature of a family. Our beliefs and values, life experiences, upbringing, and our own personal development have helped form our feelings. We reveal them as we become comfortable enough to do so. And that happens, most often, when we sense that we will be accepted for who we are.

Some people hesitate before sharing their secrets, for now or forever. People who live together before marriage are probably more likely to withhold information from each other. Moving in together is a way of testing a relationship, of seeing how it works before risking real honesty. The fear of rejection erects invisible walls of secrecy. But married people can keep secrets, too.

Let's explore the example of Ed and Kim, who were married for several years without ever enjoying a satisfying sexual relationship. There was no apparent reason for the problem. Kim was warm, affectionate, and loving—until her husband touched her in certain ways at bedtime. When he approached her physically, gentle as he was, something seemed to freeze up within her.

Ed was patient and loving, but he wondered why his wife was so unresponsive. Didn't she have sexual needs, too? Didn't she want to express her love by meeting his needs?

With great reluctance, Kim accompanied her husband to see a therapist. Several sessions seemed to go nowhere until she finally admitted, through convulsive weeping, that she was the victim of sexual abuse as a child. No one had ever discovered this happened to her. This was the first time she had ever spoken of the pain and trauma she suffered.

Suddenly Ed saw her in a new way. He embraced her and told her he understood. He promised that the two of them would face the problem together. He would better know her needs and could help her toward healing.

Clearly, Kim kept a secret. Couldn't she have told Ed a long time ago? Shouldn't she have spoken about her fears before the marriage? Of course, but imagine what went on inside this young woman. What if he rejected her?

Fear of rejection can make liars of us all.

There are many issues people are afraid to share because of that fear, that terrible possibility of not being accepted. In a perfect relationship, of course, we can tell each other everything. There are no secrets, at least in theory. However, what happens the first time I tell you something and I feel you reject me in some way? What if I tell you I have dreamed of opening a restaurant someday, and you laugh at me? What if I tell you I'm leaning toward voting for the other political party, and you roll your eyes and tell me I don't know what I'm talking about?

How do we get past this debilitating fear?

## Beyond Fear

When I ask people to name the most important element in a love relationship, the most frequent answer is *communication*. As important as that quality is, I disagree. I find that the single most important ingredient between partners is respect. If you do not respect me, you do not accept me. If you do not accept me, when I am with you I cannot be the person I really am. Instead, I have to pretend I am the picture you love.

This is why people are so afraid to be transparent with one another. Fear of rejection is the fear of losing someone, of ultimately being lonely. Therefore, when a relationship is not on sure footing, we project the picture of who we are and we hide behind it. The way we look at it, if you do not like something, I can always change the picture. However, I do not want to change the person I truly am.

*The single most important ingredient between partners is respect.*

Imagine for a moment what might have happened if Kim had approached Ed with her problem early and been rebuffed in some way. Perhaps she showed him a specially chosen movie on DVD and asked his opinion of a character that shared her (still-concealed) experience. If Ed rolled his eyes and said that the character needed to "get over it," Kim might conclude that he would never understand her problem. She would feel confirmed in her resolve to maintain the secret.

Most of us tend to be truthful until we are punished for it. The punishment may come in various forms, from ridicule to rejection to abandonment. When we confess something we have done—or confess an opinion or an emotion—and we are punished in some way, the message we receive is that it's not safe to tell the truth. Consequently, couples teach each other to lie.

Is it always comfortable to be truthful? Of course not. It can be painful to reach deep inside your heart, your soul, and share things with another person who may react negatively. It can be painful or frightening to the hearer, too, especially if they don't know how to react to the revelation. Nevertheless, pain makes honesty possible. With pain, we can continue to share; with punishment, we cannot.

So pain results in building walls made of untruths.

We all want to be accepted for who we are, without qualification. We all crave unconditional love and the freedom to tell the truth—the whole truth and nothing but the truth—and still be loved. We want another human being to know what we have done, what has been done to us, what we have fantasized about doing, and what we want for our future. We want to tell the good stories, but also the bad, the painful, and the regrettable. However, our desire to show someone the whole person, good and bad, brave and afraid, spiritual and scarred, never comes true until we trust another human being to love us in spite of everything. Until we come to that point of honesty, we will never have the relationship that will fulfill our heart's desires.

Honesty in a relationship begins with giving each other permission to be truthful. This sounds easy when, in fact, it takes a great deal of courage and can be discouraged by even a token of rejection.

Here is an example. Gary has a fear of insects. Gary is a man's man. He works out at the gym, enjoys football, and takes no foolishness from anybody. When he was five, a cruel cousin slipped a roach into his bed. He was traumatized, and to this day insects cause a panic reaction in him.

When Pam met Gary, it took a lot of coaxing to get him to go on a picnic with her. Oddly enough, he did not seem to like sitting on the ground. He could run, play football, or throw a Frisbee, but the suggestion of reclining in the grass seemed to bother him in a way Pam could not understand. After she badgered him for a while about his reasons, he told her that bugs scared him.

How did Pam react? She laughed. Long and hard. This was the manly man she was going out with? She kidded him every day for a week. Now, to Pam, it was no more than good-natured ribbing. As for Gary? He smoldered.

Pam didn't realize what she was communicating to Gary—that he had better absolutely and consistently live out the picture of a "macho man." As a result, without even realizing it, he has begun watching his words and actions, trying to live up to the image that Pam wants. Well, at least to never show weakness again and be ridiculed for it.

Do you see how subtle the pattern can be? Pam loves Gary and has no idea that she is teaching him to lie. However, that is exactly what we do in relationships when we fail to be fully accepting, even in the little things. If you reject something about me, it hurts. The whole point of our relationship is to come together, to connect. Rejection is the ultimate disconnection. Therefore, every time you fail to give me acceptance, I will redouble my efforts to avoid experiencing rejection again. I will begin painting the picture I believe you want, the one that pleases you. What I may not understand yet is how miserable I am going to be as I confine myself within this prison of dishonesty.

As you move from attraction to acceptance, then, here is your question: Can you handle the truth? Can your partner?

Are you ready to offer full acceptance, love, and respect in return for the same?

## CREATING A CLIMATE OF ACCEPTANCE

Love relationships often begin in an adrenaline rush, a too-good-to-be-true mutual adoration. If your partner seems perfect, he or she is too good to be true. But you knew that already. Slowing down, getting to know each other, and setting the right tone of honesty does not mean promptly spilling your guts about every sin you ever committed. There is no reason in the world that you should lay bare your soul on the second date. There is an appropriate time for appropriate sharing.

The best thing to do is create an atmosphere of honesty at the beginning. If you are dating someone new, simply be yourself. Rely on the person you are rather than the fantasy of some picture. Show that you are a genuine human being who is not putting on a show or hiding behind a mask.

If you are a married person, you might think this section is not for you. You may be saying, "That train left the station a long time ago." True, there should be a higher degree of honesty in your relationship by now. On the other hand, maybe there is not. How much sharing is really taking place? How transparent are you when it comes to fears, hopes, and dreams? The fact is that most couples grow closer and more honest in the beginning of a relationship, but then they might begin drifting apart. Spouses begin to collect secrets again. A wife might have dreams that she is afraid to share with her husband; he might be hiding sexual fantasies in a pornography addiction. It could be any of a million things.

If you are married, spend some time thinking about the parts of your identity that you have not been sharing. Are there areas where you need to come clean? In any relationship, new or mature, look at sharing this way: reveal your true self the way you would move through a swimming pool, from the shallow to the deep end. The shallow end is facts, as we have mentioned earlier in the chapter. Begin with the least threatening facts and build your confidence toward sharing the more difficult ones. The more threatened you feel by sharing a fact from your life, the deeper into the pool you go. Until, finally, you move from facts to the deepest end, that of your feelings, especially ones that you fear may be rejected.

So, back to our example. Gary decides he wants to stop pretending he's the macho man that Pam seems to advocate. He is going to simply be himself and let the chips fall where they may, while watching to see how Pam reacts. He sits down with her and, for the first time, shares the background of his cousin and the roach incident. She listens with fascination as he gives the factual details, but she still does not quite understand. After all, it was just a silly bug; things like that happen to children all the time, and they simply get over it.

Next, Gary begins to share the feelings that go with his facts. He tells how it felt to be away from his home and his parents, staying at his aunt's cottage in the country, and how his older cousin took advantage of the visit to pick on him. Within a few days, the cousin had so thoroughly intimidated him that young Gary was constantly looking over his shoulder, flinching when he was touched. He was half-asleep, entering a bad dream, when the roach, planted by the cousin, ran across his face and woke him with a start.

When he screeched, the cousin began laughing and calling him a little girl.

"What I felt was deep shame," Gary says. "If my cousin said I was

like a little girl, he must be right—how did I know? I was just a kid."
After that, Gary lived in fear of having his masculinity called into question.

Gary describes to Pam how, even today, anytime he observes a bully he becomes enraged. He has spent his mature years working out, competing with other athletes, and building a tough physical shell, so that no one will ever call him a sissy or a little girl again.

For the record, Pam sees Gary in a new way now. She understands what the issue of manhood means to him, and that helps her to know where his sensitive spots are. She is much more comfortable in the relationship and shows him that, for her, manhood is about integrity, courage, and dependability, all of which Gary has. She helps him work toward a healthier self-view.

As they have talked, Pam has shared a few of her own difficult childhood experiences, too. The couple feels closer to each other because they know they have shared the honest realities of their lives. There is no feeling as wonderful as that of taking off a mask and throwing it away.

*There is no feeling as wonderful as that of taking off a mask and throwing it away.*

Moving from facts to feelings has erased many tension points between couples. It will do the same for you as you build strong mutual acceptance into your relationship.

"But what if it doesn't?" you may be thinking. "What if I share these painful facts or feelings—and mine are much worse than a story about some bug—and my lover rejects me for it? What then?"

Sometimes the other person is not as accepting and understanding as Pam. I have witnessed marriages breaking up because one finally told the truth to the other, and the other simply could not or would not handle it. I am not telling you that there is no risk. There is. You have to ask yourself, "Is the risk worth it?"

Let me help you decide.

# TAKING IT TO THE LIMIT

Consider another question: "I've done some bad things. I mean really bad—but all of that was a long time ago. Do I need to turn up every single rock from my past and discuss what lies beneath it?"

The answer to this question depends upon the situation. The guiding principle is this: Does your partner feel as if he or she has free access to what you know? The freedom to know is more important than the facts that could be known.

Chad, for example, has an addictive past. His involvement with alcohol and drugs, ten years ago, put him into situations and events that now cause him regret. He has never talked to his wife, Sandra, about that period. She has only a vague knowledge of a time in his life that involved substance abuse and uncontrolled behavior.

Chad's best strategy is to let Sandra know that yes, he had a bleak period in his life, and that none of its history is off limits, unless she wants it that way. He should offer to answer honestly any question about his past. Of course, he can offer a disclaimer: "My past is not pretty, and I'm not proud of it. I have put all of that behind me, but I will tell you as much of it as you really want to know and you really believe you can handle. Keep this in mind; once I tell you, I can't untell you."

In most cases, the partner will not want to know the precise anatomy of every skeleton in the closet. What he or she will want to know is that nothing is being deliberately hidden, that any question will receive an honest answer. Most of the time that is all that is necessary to maintain a climate of honesty and acceptance.

At times, of course, curiosity will prevail. Sandra might ask something like, "What was the most dangerous drug experience you had?" She may want to know, "Do you miss the drugs?" She may really want to hear the answer, or she might simply need reassurance that she has full access to Chad and what is inside him.

The truth is that we need to continue guaranteeing this climate of honesty, just as we still need to say, "I love you." Your partner may test his or her privilege every now and then to make sure he or she still has access to whom you are.

## Where Is the Boundary?

Sometimes people in our Marriage Helper workshop insert an important question right about here: "Does respect mean that I have to accept what my mate does, as well as what my mate thinks or feels?"

The answer to that is a resounding no. We speak of respect in terms of making it safe for the other person to be himself with you—open, transparent, vulnerable. This only happens when the other person knows that you accept her as she is, "warts and all," and can love her as she is, rather than a picture she projects. That is a key to respect that must be understood and applied consistently.

*Treating the other person with respect does not mean becoming a spineless doormat.*

However, that does not mean that one has to accept every behavior the other does. Any behavior that is harmful to the individual, the spouse, the relationship, or others should not be accepted or even tolerated. It is quite all right to demand that the other stop becoming drunk, having an affair, stealing, or any other thing that meets the criteria for harmful.

Therefore, you can accept the fact that your spouse no longer feels deep love for you, and you can even accept the fact that they feel love for someone other than you. You accept feelings because for the person having those feelings, the feelings are always true, even if you do not want them to be. But it does *not* mean that you should accept your spouse committing adultery, or even spending time with the other person by phone or face to face. The key here is to separate thoughts, feelings, and actions. Accepting a person's thoughts, views, understandings, emotions, and the like means accepting that person as he is. He feels safe to be open and vulnerable, and that is the bedrock of true friendship and honest caring.

However, actions are another thing altogether.

I have no doubt that my wife loves me with all her being. She makes it possible for me to be open and honest with her about everything. And yet she would not tolerate my coming home drunk, cursing her or my family, quitting my job and becoming a bum, or any other behavior that would be detrimental to me, her, our family, our relationship, or to anyone else on the planet. If that behavior took place, she would first try to help me understand why, and would do all she could to help me stop. If it continued, despite her efforts, the woman who loves me unconditionally would not continue to allow me to live with her. It would not be that she rejected me, only that she would not accept destructive, debilitating behaviors.

That is as it should be. Treating the other person with respect does not mean becoming a spineless doormat.

## QUESTIONS – AND ANSWERS!

Though people feel their situation is unique, I hear the same questions over and over. So let's take a look at a few of these questions.

*Question: "Do I really need to answer all my spouse's questions about my affair? Some of them make me feel dirty all over again. Others make me fear that my spouse will seek revenge on the other person. Shouldn't I tell my spouse that because he or she took me back, forgiveness means never bringing it up again?"*

My answer: You will never be able to develop genuine trust in your relationship as long as your spouse knows that you are withholding information. First, telling the spouse the name of the person with whom you had the affair frees him from wondering about every man that he meets who seems to know you. He deserves that. Second, though some of his questions may be quite painful to hear answers to—and may not even be good for his own mental and emotional health—if you hide it from him, he will not trust you again. While it is not ideal, it is necessary. If your spouse has forgiven you for something terrible, then truth, honesty, and transparency are crucial to restoring that relationship.

The good news is that as your spouse learns the entire truth, he will, with time, forgive, and accept you again. You know that he or she loves the person, not just the picture.

*Question: "But what if I've done something bad that my spouse doesn't know about. Should I tell her that?"*

My answer: I base my response to this one on the principle of telling your spouse what builds her up according to her need. In my estimation, you can decide if your spouse needs to hear about an indiscretion or problem that he or she does not know about by answering the following three questions.

1. Is there any other way your spouse can find out? If so, you need to be the one to tell him or her about it. While it will hurt to hear it, it will hurt much more if your spouse hears it from someone else.

2. Has your spouse ever asked and you lied? This entire chapter is about the love that comes through honesty, openness, and transparency. If you have told a lie in the past, you will always have that hanging over your head and in your heart, keeping you from having the deepest love possible with your spouse. If there is a lie buried within, expose it by telling the truth.

3. Is there any part of you that you hold back because of fear, shame, guilt, or any other emotion resulting from what you have done? If so, your spouse has the right to know what it is that keeps you from being as close as he or she wants and needs you to be. Knowing what is keeping you distant is much less painful and fearful than wondering what is making you distant emotionally. Tell the truth so that each of you can now work on the problem.

*Question: "What if my spouse rejects me when I tell the truth? She might even divorce me!"*

My answer: The truth is that your spouse may well throw you out, reject you, or even divorce you. However, if you tell your spouse the truth and he or she talks of ending the marriage, give us a call. Couples who attend our Marriage Helper weekend workshop come because they are in trouble. Our success rate over several years is that three of every four couples who attend the workshop turn their marriage around, learn to overcome the past, and make a great future together. Find out more about it at www.MarriageHelper.com.

Maybe the simplest way to decide if you want to be truthful in your relationship is to ask yourself one simple question: Do you want to live as you are living now for the rest of your life?

If you like secrecy and shutting your spouse out of certain information, then you may want to keep your relationship as it is for the rest of your life. However, there are two downsides to consider. First, your spouse may not be nearly as accepting of this emotional distance as you are. Second, you are missing what could be the most wonderful relationship that you could ever imagine. I cannot begin to tell you the number of times a marriage has gotten better after a crisis where one violated the other's trust. It was not the violation that made the marriage stronger, but the courage finally to tell the truth. That caused pain, without doubt, but as the couple worked through it, they reached a level of intimacy they'd never had before. Why? Because now their relationship has true acceptance of the people themselves—with all their blemishes and scars—rather than of the pictures projected.

Just as attraction comes at the beginning of a relationship and must continue, acceptance is established near the beginning and must continue. When the time comes that you have wandered off the LovePath, check the acceptance factor. When it is fully established, you will find yourself "back in cycle," once again experiencing the joy of total acceptance and moving irresistibly into the next phase: *attachment*.

### CHAPTER SUMMARY

*The second step of the LovePath is acceptance.*

We want to be loved for the person we really are rather than the picture that we paint for others to see. In a relationship the most important thing is respect—accepting the other as he or she is, in thoughts, actions, and emotions, without trying to control or manipulate any of those areas.

To know more about yourself, write answers to the question, *what do I expect from a relationship?* if single, or, if in a relationship, *what do I expect from this relationship?*

*To develop the deepest levels of acceptance, openly share the facts and feelings of your life.*

Start with the nonthreatening and, as trust develops, move to the more threatening. People tend to share openly until they are punished. Give your lover permission to tell the truth.

When deciding whether to share something that your partner does not know, ask yourself three questions:

- Is there any other way he or she can find out? It hurts less to hear it from you.
- Has he or she ever asked? Get lies off the table for true intimacy.
- Is there any part of yourself that you hold back because of fear, shame, guilt, or any other negative emotion associated with the thing you wonder if you should tell? If so, it may well be worth it to take the risk.

# WHY WE FALL MADLY IN LOVE

*Lovesick. There was* no other word for it.

Jeremy thought he must be losing his mind. After all, he had never been the sentimental type. He hated those romantic hearts-and-roses movies, the chick flicks that his girlfriends made him watch. As far as he was concerned, he would rather have a root canal than tune his car radio to one of those stations that played cheesy love ballads.

He had always believed that so-called romantic love was a myth created by Hollywood, Hallmark, and Harlequin romance novels. At the very least, it was a game played by overly dramatic high school girls. Certainly not mature adults. For Jeremy, love was an intentional, rational process. You saw a member of the opposite sex whom you found attractive. You found out whether or not your personalities made a good mix. Ultimately you made a contract to link arms and do life together.

Or not.

Forget the sappy, head-over-heels stuff. Love was about, well, sensible shopping.

Now, here he was living out every romantic cliché in the book!

Jeremy had been out with fifteen or twenty different young ladies since eleventh grade. Dating had been a good time for the most part, sometimes a bit more formal and serious than others. With one of his steady girlfriends, Barbara, he had even used the word *love*. That was a couple of years ago, when he was twenty-five. At the time, he believed he was more or less in love with Barbara.

However, his feelings for her, during the eighteen months of that relationship, were nothing like the nuclear-powered emotions he now felt for Trish. Just thinking about Trish actually made his chest hurt. What was *that* all about?

The whole Trish situation had become almost overpowering to him. He couldn't concentrate on his job as an accountant. His thoughts kept returning to Trish, Trish, and more Trish, no matter how much he concentrated on getting on with his life and his work. At night, he tossed and turned in bed, thinking about her, agonizing about whether she returned his love, examining and reexamining every word of their most recent conversation.

When he sent Trish flowers, she responded with a thank-you card that contained five polite sentences. He micro-analyzed those sentences, searching for some subtle item of evidence of Trish's passion, until he committed every word to memory. He would fall asleep in the certainty that indeed things were going well, that surely the love was overflowing on her side as it was on his. Then he would wake up, decide it was all an illusion, and his chest would begin aching again.

Jeremy marveled that Trish, at twenty-six, was still single. There was no one like her in the world, anywhere. Why weren't the 3.3 billion males on this planet making a mad rush at her? Yet his friends looked puzzled when he rhapsodized over her perfection. They thought she was a nice girl and everything, but . . .

He walked out of an office meeting on an impulse to go see Trish in her own office, which was some thirty minutes away at this time of day. His boss wasn't likely to understand, but he didn't care. He had to see Trish!

In the past a girl need not do much more than look at him the wrong way, and that was enough to send him packing. Sometimes he broke it off, and sometimes the girl did so, but never had he really fought for someone's love. Even on the three or four occasions when he liked the girl a lot, he gave up the pursuit at the slightest resistance.

The Trish situation was different. She made it clear early on that she was not serious about Jeremy. Maybe she would go out with him again, but she wanted to date other men. Hearing those words increased Jeremy's passion. If anything, it stoked his fire until he was more determined than ever to win her love. He marveled at his own determination.

Yes, it seemed all those love songs and chick flicks were true after all. Maybe there was even a little winged cupid flying around with a bow. His arrow seemed to have hit Jeremy and gone all the way through, because he had never felt such strong emotions about anything in life.

Hey, was he even still Jeremy?

## UNDERSTANDING LIMERENCE

Limerence. Have you ever heard of it? Don't worry; it is a new term even to some who study human behavior.

Dorothy Tennov, a psychology professor, coined the word in 1977. She was interested in what happened when two people fell intensely in love. Was there a pattern? Was it a romantic delusion inspired by sentimental pop culture? Would we find the same love experience, say, across the world in China?

Most of Tennov's research came from thousands of personal accounts of those who had fallen in love. She discovered that many who considered themselves "madly in love" had similar descriptions of their emotions and actions. She chose the label *limerence* to describe an intense longing and desire for another person that is much stronger than a simple infatuation, but not the same as a long-lived love that could last a lifetime.

*Limerence is often overpowering, and in intense cases will cause a person to be obsessed with the one they've fallen for.*

Limerence is often overpowering, and in intense cases will cause a person to be obsessed with the one they've fallen for. Be sure to note that limerence is not a step on the LovePath, but a condition that may or may not exist as one navigates the LovePath. Some people experience it. Others do not. The level of intensity for those who do experience it varies.

Limerence can be euphoric, which is not a bad thing if the people who feel it for each other have no obstacles to their relationship. If they firmly establish their relationship, limerence fades in its intensity and, hopefully, will be replaced by a calmer, deeper type of love. However, if one or both are in a committed relationship with someone else, limerence can blind them to their original commitments and lead them to abandon their mates for the new love. Also, limerence can blind one to the flaws in the other so that they don't realize how bad the new relationship might be until the limerence has faded.

You've likely known someone who was headstrong and determined to marry a person whom everyone else could see was not good for him or her. At the outset, they had bliss because of the limerence. When limerence faded, they realized what a terrible mistake they had made.

Limerence brings people together—passionately. However, it never *keeps* them together. That's why it's so important to learn the art not only of falling in love but also of staying in love. Inevitably, limerence goes away. If the relationship does not have a sound foundation other than the original intense emotions, it is nearly always doomed.

Therefore, limerence is not a goal of the LovePath, and sometimes is an unwelcome storm to struggle through as you grow on the Love-Path. It can be good—and often is—but as indicated above, it can be very bad.

Allow me to illustrate.

Imagine two people in a culture where parents arrange marriages in a very formal, businesslike way. Everyone, including the young couple, accepts the marital deal as a matter of course. The husband and wife find each other pleasant. Indeed they experience attraction and, later on, mutual acceptance. They will spend the rest of their lives together with wonderful dedication to each other, and form a deep, loving bond. However, it is unlikely that either of them will ever fall "head over heels" in love in the sense that Jeremy did.

How, then, does limerence fit on the LovePath for them?

For this couple, it does not. That is one of the factors that makes this concept unique. It is a rather dramatic event that comes and goes. It is a phenomenon that may occur as we walk along the LovePath, but it is not part of the path itself. That is why passionate, emotional, overwhelming love will be such an important part of the experience for some, and practically nonexistent for others. As a matter of fact, Jeremy may go on to marry Trish without her ever experiencing the crazy emotions he has gone through.

Limerence comes somewhere during the attraction and acceptance phases, and, as you can already imagine (particularly if you've ever "caught" this particular bug), it plays havoc with a person's life and love. Consider this: scientists have begun to study the brain during what we are identifying as limerence. During this state, there are elevated levels of central dopamine and norepinephrine and decreased levels of central serotonin. The effects are euphoric and can actually be addictive (hang on to that thought for later). Dopamine increases feelings of pleasure. Serotonin is a chemical that helps us bond with another. It also helps to calm us and normally helps with restraint and inhibitions. One of the facets of limerence is at least some fear that the relationship may not endure. If serotonin were at normal levels, that fear might be alleviated to some degree. With decrease of fear comes a corresponding decrease in the intensity of passion. Additionally, as serotonin decreases while dopamine and norepinephrine increase, a person behaves in a less controlled manner and with fewer inhibitions.

*When we fall powerfully in love, we get what we might call an emotional "rush," a natural high (dopamine).*

I am simplifying scientific research a little too much here, but I want to make the point that what is happening in the brain is why lovesick individuals do some of the crazy things they do.

Put it all together. When we fall powerfully in love, we get what we might call an emotional "rush," a natural high (dopamine). Meanwhile, nature turns off the safety device (serotonin) that keeps us from doing anything crazy. That lack of serotonin makes us more fearful of losing the lover, which increases the intensity of the passion and obsession.

Think about Jeremy, who has a hard time even recognizing his own behavior. He feels the chemical reaction in his brain kicking in, and he likes how that feels. He will read Trish's letter repeatedly, convincing himself of her love to keep the good feeling flowing (not that he realizes that is what he is doing). Then, since his personal serotonin fuel gauge is lower than normal, he finds himself doing crazy things he would never do in any other circumstance.

So how is someone experiencing limerence likely to behave? If it has ever happened to you, you will recognize the signs.

## A Field Guide to Limerence

In 2002, Helen Fisher, PhD, in concert with other researchers, published the article "Defining the Brain Systems of Lust, Romantic Attraction, and Attachment" in the *Archives of Sexual Behavior*. Considered a leading researcher of what draws people together and how the process evolves from a general need to attachment to a specific person, she and her research colleagues have identified several characteristics of a person who is "madly in love," or, as we put it, in limerence. (The word *limerent* refers to the person in limerence. The phrase *limerent object* refers to the person that the limerent has limerence for.)

We paraphrase the thirteen characteristics below.

1. The limerent sets the limerent object apart from the rest of the world. Limerence sets its sights on one, and only one, object of adoration. It is impossible to experience limerence with more than one person at a time.

2. The limerent sees the limerent object only in a positive light, and the negatives become invisible. Even the things associated with that person—letters, words, events—are cherished and adored as being "special" because they are associated with the limerent object.

*The limerent may obsessively think about the limerent object, up to 85 percent of waking hours.*

3. The limerent's life becomes crazy from a physical and emotional point of view. He typically experiences things such as euphoria, energy surges, insomnia, loss of appetite, abrupt mood swings, or rapid heartbeat. She may experience anxiety, panic, or fear in the presence of the limerent object.

4. In times of adversity, the limerent feels even stronger emotions for and attraction to the limerent object.

5. The limerent may obsessively think about the limerent object, up to 85 percent of waking hours. Psychologists call it "intrusive thinking."

6. The limerent typically exhibits signs of emotional dependency on the relationship with the limerent object, including possessiveness, jealousy, fear of rejection, and separation anxiety. (Tennov points out that because of this, limerents tend to perceive anyone who may keep them from the limerent object as an enemy.)

7. The limerent feels a deep longing for emotional union with the limerent object.

8. The limerent feels a powerful sense of empathy toward the limerent object and is willing to sacrifice for her.

9. The limerent tends to reorder her daily priorities. The limerent may change the way he dresses, and change mannerisms or habits to become more attractive to the limerent object. She may change values to be more available for the limerent object.

10. The limerent feels sexual desire for the limerent object. This desire is coupled with possessiveness, a strong drive for sexual exclusivity, and feelings of jealousy or fear of competition from others.

11. And yet the limerent craves emotional union more strongly than sexual union with the limerent object.

12. The limerent feels that he cannot control the emotions felt for the limerent object. Limerents commonly report their passion is involuntary and uncontrollable.

13. Limerence is impermanent. It eventually subsides. However, it may take longer to subside if physical or social barriers inhibit the limerent partners from seeing each other regularly.

Did you catch that last one? If you have ever experienced the power and the passion of this romantic attraction, you know the truth of it: limerence feels like forever, but it runs its course.

When?

Studies indicate that it will last anywhere from six months to three years. However, according to Tennov, there are three things, besides the passing of time, that cause limerence to cease:

1. *Consummation.* The bliss of reciprocation is gradually either blended into a lasting love or replaced by less positive feelings.
2. *Starvation.* The beloved does not return the limerence; finally the person in limerence has to admit that there is no reciprocation.
3. *Transformation.* The person in limerence moves on to another person to love, no longer feeling the limerence toward the previous beloved.

The study of this phenomenon is still relatively new. Social scientists continue to research, and to compare the notes they have taken on those who have been through the storm of romantic infatuation. Other scientists hook up their wires, employ functional MRI pictures, read their meters, and tell us what the brain is up to during that amazing period.

The more we learn, the more clearly we understand what is going on: we are experiencing the powerful human need to find one specific mate, to be fruitful and to multiply, to fill the earth (in the language of the book of Genesis). The process must be irresistible for at least some so that we will keep furnishing the earth with new generations. It is a kind of biological conspiracy in which all the parts of your body participate, right down to the unseen happenings in your brain. When they occur, these processes unite to drive us toward one special person. Like Jeremy, we feel the thrill of a hundred roller-coaster rides; the dopamine makes us feel good, and the lack of serotonin makes us feel invulnerable. We will do crazy things to claim the lover of our dreams.

It is wonderful, isn't it? So romantic!

Well, not exactly. Not always. There is a reason this book is *The Art of Falling in Love* rather than *The Art of Falling in Limerence*. Let us explore the darker side of limerence.

## Love, Limerence, and Timing

Let us return to lovesick Jeremy. We wanted Trish to return his love and for the two of them to live happily ever after. Why not? We were talking about two unattached people. However, what if limerence were to explode once again in Jeremy's life, or in Trish's, for that matter? What if it happened ten years later, after they married, started a family, and settled into their lives?

Yes, it's true. Limerence can strike the same person again, and it does not necessarily recognize marriage certificates. Cupid can be reckless in his aim, and he might fire an arrow at someone who is already "spoken for." Limerence may well kick in right in the middle of a marriage, and not toward the marriage partner, but toward someone else.

Thousands of extramarital affairs begin exactly this way.

Jeremy eventually won his bride. Marrying Trish was the happiest day of his life, and the emotional honeymoon lasted for about a year. After that, all was peaceful; Jeremy got back to being the quiet, dependable certified public accountant he had always been. Thank goodness for that, because if he had continued in that emotionally topsy-turvy state of mind, his career might have been derailed.

Trish fell in love; limerence, not so much. Jeremy's passion and persistence had simply won her over, and now she was committed to him. Children came, there was a larger house, and all was well.

Unfortunately that's when Melinda entered the picture.

Melinda was a younger accountant in the firm. She and Jeremy were assigned to the same client over a six-month period, where they worked closely together to perform in-house audits. They would ride to the site in Jeremy's car, and then spend hours crunching the numbers side by side.

Well, you guessed it. There was attraction on both sides. Nothing wrong there; it can happen to the best of us. We stand in an elevator and notice some great-looking individual, but we do not follow them down the hall. Minutes later we have forgotten all about that person, no matter how attractive he or she might have been. While attraction is the first step on the LovePath, temporary passing attraction is not actually on that step.

However, strong attraction—to the point that we continue thinking about the person to whom we are attracted—is a start on the LovePath, whether we mean it to be or not. For most of us, we abandon that almost as soon as it hits and leave the LovePath with that person. If we do not, we are on the LovePath and will continue on it until something moves us off.

*The LovePath is the way of genuine love. It is our map to building a healthy life of romantic attachment.*

For example, what would happen if we spent hours with a person we were attracted to and found ourselves sharing the details of our daily lives, our dreams, and our feelings? We are definitely on the LovePath, though if anyone asked, we would deny it. Lying? Probably not, just being naïve. That is why some are on the LovePath without realizing it. If they were to move from attraction to acceptance, they would move to the serious second step of the Love-Path. There is still time to get off the path if the person so chooses. Limerence, however, could become the wild card that spins it out of control. It intensifies everything we feel so that we allow ourselves to be drawn into something we know is dangerous.

Jeremy loved his wife and his marriage was good, even if a certain amount of passion had drained away. He never intended to fall in love with Melinda, but suddenly he was experiencing all the feelings and drives he had experienced with Trish. After several years' absence, here came those surges through his brain. He had forgotten how good they felt. In addition, with the low ebb of serotonin that would tend to inhibit his actions, he found himself very careless. How could he allow himself to be seen eating in a restaurant with Melinda, three blocks from home? People do reckless things when they are having affairs and their bodies are low on serotonin levels.

Pay close attention to the next two statements, because they are among the most important ones in this book:

*The LovePath is the way of genuine love.* It is our map to building a healthy life of romantic attachment.

*Limerence is not long-lasting love.* It may be a part of the love experience, but it is fickle and treacherous. If unchecked, it can set in at the wrong place and the wrong time.

## MASTERING LIMERENCE

What can we do about limerence? That is a big question, because it is a challenge as old as the human race.

Limerence is not evil. After all, it marks the beginning of many wonderful relationships. In the right situation, it creates drama, romance, and beautiful memories.

On the flip side, though, it is not always beneficial. Limerence can set in when we have stopped caring for our primary love relationship, and when we allow ourselves to be pulled onto the LovePath with an inappropriate partner. Perhaps the most enduring devastation of limerence is that it causes us to confuse intense emotions with long-lived love.

Let's take one more look at the case of Jeremy, Trish, and Melinda.

Jeremy remembered his recent self-assurance that he had a good, solid marriage with Trish. He also remembered—and missed—the incredible rush of romantic feelings early in their relationship. Trish missed it, too. She missed the unexpected roses, the gentle words of passion, and the single-minded dedication that Jeremy once showed. She clung to her own heart's love, which was not as overwhelmingly passionate, but was sure and steady.

What Jeremy decided was that he must have "fallen out of love" with his wife, and here was the genuine article returning in his feelings toward Melinda. In time he began to do what most people do when they want out of a marriage. He began to rewrite history in his memory so that the level of limerence he once felt for Trish evaporated. He did not remember it any longer and he felt that with Melinda, for the first time, he was truly in love. He also became convinced that his life with Trish was not happy over the years. In his mental rewriting, he gradually forgot good times and focused on bad. Finally, he said, "I love Trish like a sister, but I'm not in love with her. I'm in love with Melinda. This is the love I've wanted and longed for all my life."

He did not know about limerence, but the feeling was so powerful, and it was so consistent with the cultural idea of romance, that he believed it must be love. After all, who was he to fight the irresistible force of true love?

He also did something that Tennov mentioned in her studies, and that I have noticed in every person with limerence: he viewed all those who stood between him and Melinda as his enemies. Including Trish. As his wife, she was an obstacle to his having Melinda. His pastor and others at his church also became enemies because they tried to intervene and get him to save his marriage rather than destroy it. In his eyes even his own parents became enemies because they urged him to stay with Trish and stop the relationship with Melinda.

Via limerence emotions masquerading as logic, he rationalized that his parents would eventually get over it, and that those who were his true friends would come around. He convinced himself that God sent Melinda, and those hypocrites at church could not see it because they placed their rules over God's love.

Jeremy left his wife and rented an apartment with Melinda. It caused heartbreak at home and a scandal at work. His company would not allow them to work together, so Melinda had to find another job. The couple felt that all the pain was validated by their "courageous" choice to be together. Obstacles drew them closer together; it was the two of them against the world.

What do you think happened after time passed? Limerence ran its course, as it always does. Jeremy came more or less back to his senses. Gradually he could not understand why he had gone so insane over Melinda, why he had given up everything to have her. He saw her flaws, which had not seemed to have been there before, and found himself wondering how in the world he had gotten into this mess. What was wrong with him, anyway?

Melinda did not lose limerence when Jeremy did. Rather than moving on, she did what limerent objects typically do when they realize that their lover is pulling away. She did everything she could think of to keep him from leaving her. She begged. She threatened to ruin his reputation. She became sick and claimed she needed him to be with her. She blamed him for getting her into the situation and then abandoning her to be alone and lonely. She told him where her life could have been if she had never met him. She called him names, accused him of stealing part of her life, and wept copiously in his arms. She did not go as far as some people have—namely, resorting to violence—but she did enough to make it very, very hard for Jeremy to leave her.

What about Trish? She was not so certain that she wanted Jeremy back. The kids, of course, wanted their father. After insisting upon certain conditions, Trish finally accepted a reconciliation. But there was a great deal of work for Jeremy to do in marriage counseling, in fence mending with his kids, in forgiving and understanding himself, and in restoring the respect he had worked so hard to earn at the office.

Yes, limerence is like a drug. It is a powerful high, but the hangover can be painful. Jeremy knew nothing of love paths or limerence. He was a good man who had done a bad thing that, at the time, he convinced himself was not bad at all. He came home, began working hard on being a good husband and father, and it is unlikely that he will ever make the same mistake again.

What about men and women who are less fortunate or wise? What about the ones who do not come home?

Some of them become addicted to the drug. They leave a home in shambles, fail to forgive or come to terms with their own emotions, and run off into the sunset to chase the next high. We know there are people who have addictive personalities, and who struggle to overcome their craving for stimulation. Love, or more precisely limerence, can become one more destructive narcotic. It consumes some people who become serial monogamists, moving from one short-term relationship to another, using people as a way to get that emotional high.

## BACK ON THE PATH

What about you? Have you ever fallen truly, madly, deeply in love? Do you recognize the symptoms we have reviewed in this chapter? Perhaps you even bought this book because you are lovesick, completely taken with another person and bewildered by what is happening to your life and mind.

It is not as if the surge of powerful passion will subside the moment you discover what it is. Nevertheless, it helps to understand what is going on in your body and in your mind. It is good to know that your perspective on the one you love is skewed in a falsely positive direction, and that you may behave in uninhibited ways. It is also empowering to understand that your feelings will not last forever. That you can choose not to act on them.

Therefore, if you are already married, or perhaps you have fallen in love with someone who is, understand that you will not forever think and feel as you do now. In a few months, maybe a couple years, you could be looking upon the ruins of many lives, including your own. These are important factors to consider.

The weakest point of limerence is its lack of durability. Six to thirty-six months can be a long time, but it is not forever. Are you willing to give up what you believe in, who you are, and what you have accomplished for a few months of euphoria before reality sets in?

# A SPOUSE IN LIMERENCE WITH SOMEONE ELSE

Spouses who are left by a husband or wife in limerence often ask me what to do. I tell them to think of their spouse as an addict and treat him or her as one.

Sometimes you can simply wait it out. For example, a woman in Trish's position might be served with divorce papers, even though she still feels the marriage is worth fighting for (Jeremy, again, is a good person who has done a bad thing). It is in her interest to stall the legal process of divorce as long as she can. In time, the chances are good that limerence will run its course and Jeremy will become himself again.

Of course, because Jeremy is in limerence he will be as manipulative as any other addict. He will cajole, make promises, threaten, and make life miserable for her if she does not do as he wishes and make it easier for him to be with Melinda. However, I would still advise Trish to drag it out if she wants any chance of getting Jeremy back. If she still hopes for a future with Jeremy, one way to fight is to drag it out as long as possible. Time is on her side and against him. Limerence *will* fade. She has to decide if she is willing to fight for her marriage and wait until limerence dies.

On the other hand, if she decides she does not want Jeremy back, she can make it easy and let him go.

Sometimes you need to do an intervention as you would with any other addict. If you wish to know how to do that, you can download an article I have written on the subject (go to www.JoeBeam.com/Intervention.htm).

## *Unreciprocated Limerence*

A question I hear often from singles is, "What if you fall head-over-heels for someone, but she simply doesn't return your feelings?" I remind you that this too shall pass. No matter what I tell you right now, it seems to you that your heart will break if your beloved does not respond to your overtures. You are absolutely convinced that there are not a lot of fish in the sea, at least not like the fish for whom you have set your hook! Believe me, you will not always feel the same way you do now. Time heals all wounds (and perhaps wounds all heels).

## LIMERENCE VERSUS THE LOVEPATH

Now, consider the difference between limerence and genuine love.

- Limerence is a tempestuous turmoil of emotions and urges, but lifelong love is made of stronger, more enduring stuff.
- Limerence sets in almost overnight, but lifelong love is built over months, years, a lifetime.
- Limerence makes you become someone else, but lifelong love makes you become a better version of yourself.

On the LovePath, you begin with attraction. Whether or not your brain begins its crazy dance called limerence, if you continue to fall in love, you move on to acceptance. You begin to move beyond the perceived picture of someone to the true person who lies behind it. To a love that is more honest and accurate than limerence, which touches up the best features and hides the worst.

The LovePath leads to *attachment*, and in that lies the possibility of the deepest joys of true union. There is no time limit, no window of a few months or a couple of years. Love will endure throughout life, opening up into ever deeper and more fulfilling possibilities to be shared them together.

Therefore, regardless of fairy tales, TV movies, or *Cosmo* articles, the love that satisfies, fulfills, and makes life wonderful is not the tempestuous state of limerence, but the bonded, long-lived relationship found in fulfilled attachment.

Attachment is where true love lives.

Finally, limerence is a power that overcomes us, but lifelong love is a gift that overwhelms us. Limerence is a natural force, but love, which is selfless and sacrificial, comes from a supernatural source. It offers us a path, and we can follow that path toward those deeper levels of satisfaction. When we wander off the path, when we lose our way, we can always find our way back onto it again. We can enhance our attractiveness, broaden our acceptance, and strengthen our attachment to fall in love all over again. Fall in limerence again? No, something deeper and longer lasting.

Love is not a feeling that is out of our hands, but a pathway we are always free to follow.

## CHAPTER SUMMARY

*The state of feeling "madly in love" is what we refer to as limerence.*
- Limerence is euphoric but not forever.
- Limerence is not a step on the LovePath, but a condition that may or may not exist as one travels the LovePath.
- Limerence is associated with the increase of certain brain chemicals and the decrease of others. That results in at least thirteen characteristics of a person in limerence, including feelings of euphoria and a lack of boundaries and inhibitions. Therefore, limerence may be a storm blowing one off the LovePath with one person onto the path with another.

*Limerence ends in one of three ways:*
- *Consummation*—it either blends into lasting love or is replaced by less positive feelings.
- *Starvation*—limerence is unreciprocated; the person feeling it finally admits it doesn't exist in the beloved.
- *Transformation*—the person in limerence moves on to another person to love.

*Limerence will not last.*
- Typically, limerence occurs for six to thirty-six months and then dissipates. Whether single or married, a person making life decisions based on what he or she feels in limerence may well end up with unhappy consequences and deep regrets.

# STEP THREE:
# ATTACHMENT

# THE STAGE OF
# COMMITMENT

*We all want* a fairy-tale romance, don't we? We imagine ourselves as the handsome prince and the beautiful princess, riding off into the sunset on a white stallion. Maybe that horse has a bumper sticker that reads, "Happily Ever After."

Who doesn't want storybook love? When we are still in diapers, our parents begin telling us tales from the Happily Ever After file. Of course, if those children's stories were a little more realistic, I guess the Brothers Grimm would be much grimmer. Goldilocks, for example, would get safely away from those three bears, but she would grow up without ever finding the right man. She would come home from every date with a frown on her face, saying, "That one was too hot!" or, "That one was too cold!" Never, "Just right!"

Okay, I am about to get a little absurd in this next illustration, but it is a great way to explain the difference between limerence and attachment. Think for a moment about Prince Charming. We thought he was going to settle down after he scoured the neighborhood to find Cinderella, the one who fit the slipper. But Prince Charming later turns up to lay a big kiss on Sleeping Beauty, to awaken her and claim another

Happily Ever After. Then, more than pleased with himself, he uses the same formula with Snow White, another late sleeper, for yet another Happily Ever After.

If we apply what we have learned in the last few chapters, we can make a strong case that the good prince has developed a craving for the dopamine rush of limerence. We might call him a limerence addict. He first experienced it with Cinderella, obsessing over her after she fled at the stroke of midnight. He examined that glass slipper repeatedly because it belonged to the one he loved. Its foot odor was perfume to him, and her absence only increased the intensity of his passion. As his serotonin levels decreased, he began to act irrationally, spending countless dollars from his royal budget on door-to-door shoe fittings.

Then, having found his woman, he lived Happily Ever After . . . for six to thirty-six months. By then, of course, he had met Sleeping Beauty and started the cycle all over again. I imagine that when he got home and broke the news to Cinderella, he told her, "My name is Charming, not Dependable."

*There is certainly no call for us to build emotional defenses against falling in love just because the limerence rush does not last.*

Real life, of course, is a little messier, a little less perfect than fairy tales. Even so, we become childlike again when we meet someone special. Falling in love is the moment in life that feels the most like a fairy tale.

Have you ever rushed into romance a little too starry eyed? Believed the feel-good emotions would carry you through the rest of life? Clearly, that's not so. And yet, we don't need to become cynical or distrusting. There is certainly no call for us to build emotional defenses against falling in love just because the limerence rush does not last.

What, then, should we do? Simple: understand how love works and how it can be built to last. These next few chapters help you understand the third step on the LovePath, which we call *attachment*. This is the true merger, when two people become one, making a wholehearted commitment to a relationship. As we do that, and as we make the right decisions together, we really do find our lives merging in important ways.

We began with attraction, and our descriptive word was *closer.*

We moved on to acceptance, and we agreed that it was all about *caring.*

Finally, we come to attachment. The theme this time is *commitment.*

When you think of the "c" word, what may come to mind is the idea of making a decision. We make a commitment to keep an appointment somewhere. We make a financial commitment to donate money to a charity or a church. We make spiritual commitments to some form of faith. Pure decision is a powerful thing, because we are saying, "This is who I am going to be; this is what I'm going to do." When we commit ourselves to a future with one other person, we are removing tentativeness and uncertainty from the relationship. Perhaps we are even saying that we will stand up in a church or some other public place and make a solemn vow to keep that commitment in sickness and in health, for better or for worse, from this day forward.

As we have often heard, the road to hell is often paved with good intentions, well-meaning commitments. We need something more than a bare promise and a good intention to make a relationship work. It can be the road to mutual joy (the LovePath), or it can indeed become a road to what feels like hell on earth.

Let's explore what happens—in our bodies, minds, and spirits—when, long after the first rush of romance has given way, we deepen our attachment to our beloved.

## THE VALUE OF ATTACHMENT

On the LovePath, attachment and its attendant commitment are the goals of lifelong love. It is not the fire of limerence, which burns so bright but extinguishes so quickly, that is the goal. It is the bonding that takes place in attachment. Although it may not always be exciting, it is always fulfilling. So if your desire is real love, rather than seeking the thrill of fairy tales, pursue the long-lasting, though less emotionally intoxicating, bonded love of attachment.

So many times I have worked with couples where one would say something such as, "He's my best friend. But there just is not the romance I crave. I have to have that." Then I watch as this person leaves her best friend to seek the Prince Charming of her dreams.

Never have I seen it work out well.

Sure, the thrill of heated romance fulfills—for a while. But seemingly without exception, these people end up sad that they sacrificed their best friend for a romantic feeling that felt so wonderful yet subsided with time.

Rather than buy into the love touted in movies and novels, one would do so much *better*—and have a much more fulfilling life across the years—if he or she understood that the goal of human coupling is not excitement, but a deep, abiding contentment that comes from fulfillment. It is not a constant thrill, but rather a lifelong acceptance. It is not a fluttering stomach and constant intrusive thinking of the beloved, but an assurance that there is one person who loves you, day in and day out, who will always accept you as you are, and who will stand beside you no matter what. It is this love that people crave as they grow older and have a much wiser perspective of life. Which makes it so sad that, far too often, this love is what they throw away when they are young and seeking fairy tales rather than reality.

## THE HUMAN BODY

Science continues to bring us wonderful new discoveries about our bodies and what happens inside them throughout the experience of love. We have already seen, for example, how chemicals "conspire" to increase our passion and decrease our inhibitions when we fall madly in love.

There are also a number of intriguing findings about the attachment between husbands and wives in committed relationships. For example, we know about oxytocin, a hormone in our bodies that increases trust and bonding. When a mother is breast-feeding, her brain releases oxytocin so that she and her baby bond. There is a beauty in the way nature feeds our physical and emotional needs simultaneously.

However, the infant-mother bond is not the only way this chemical does its work.

Oxytocin is involved in the inducement of labor when the mother is about to give birth. During the delivery, there is an oxytocin surge in both parents (assuming the father is present) so that a powerful bond between mother, father, and child is created. If you are a parent, you remember that moment when you first saw your newborn. You would have climbed any mountain or swam any sea for your new child because of this powerful connection.

However, let us remove parenting from the equation for a moment. Science also has discovered that oxytocin levels are increased when we are affectionate with a partner. Cuddling, gentle touch, positive words, and other expressions of our love—all of these create chemistry between us. There is a particularly strong rush of oxytocin during sexual intercourse at the point of orgasm. Yes, it happens in both the male and the female; attachment chemistry is an equal-opportunity feel-good process.

The list of benefits of this hormone is astounding. A good steady flow of oxytocin calms stress and anxiety. It reduces cravings, including those for drugs and alcohol. Its presence seems to be involved with medications that combat depression.

*A good hug, a kind word, and regularly making love to one's spouse are good medicine.*

Think about it this way: you might go to the gym for positive physical health benefits; you can also love someone for positive mental, physical, and emotional health benefits. Studies have shown for years that those who are committed in attachment to others, especially in marriage, tend to live longer and have fewer medical issues. A good hug, a kind word, and regularly making love to one's spouse are good medicine. These simple pleasures fight cravings, unhealthy dependencies, and even common depression.

There is more. Barry McCarthy, PhD, refers to a large U.S. study that indicates that 20 percent of married couples between the ages of eighteen and fifty-nine have sex ten times per year or less. These marriages are called No Sex Marriages. An additional 15 percent of married couples in that same demographic in America have sex with each other eleven to twenty-five times per year. These marriages are called Low Sex Marriages. Why is that important? Several medical findings indicate that the healthiest pattern for a husband and wife is to have orgasmic lovemaking regularly. When this happens, men are at a reduced risk for fatal heart attacks, women are less likely to have a heart attack, and men have fewer occurrences of prostate cancer.

When a couple makes love, they increase their attachment and mutual trust without even realizing it. The marriage gets stronger because their bond gets stronger.

Attachment makes people better caregivers, not only for their mates but also for other people, including their children. Strong attachment helps people cope with stress. It simply makes them healthier, more effective human beings.

Isn't love a wonderful thing?

Think about it. The initial rush of limerence is passionate enough to send us chasing after someone we want, but we could never sustain that level of passion. We would obsess over each other forever, we would be emotionally intoxicated, and we would have few inhibitions. The world would be in trouble! Humans would have died out long ago because rather than planting crops or raising animals, everyone in limerence would be under a tree kissing their beloved. It makes sense that we are designed to sustain that level of desire for a limited period.

Then, we begin the process of lifelong attachment. It is less about hearts, flowers, and uncontrolled passion, and more about touches, conversations, and genuine friendship. In both stages, the chemicals do their thing, whether it is to push us into action or to keep us knit tightly together. Limerence cannot last, but genuine attachment maintains itself for a lifetime.

When a man and woman make love, they experience a dopamine rush, just as they did during limerence. After the act is concluded, that dopamine level bottoms out. If the couple does not possess a true commitment, the result is they will turn immediately away from each other. Emptiness lingers and propels the need to go after more relatively empty stimulation later.

In true, loving attachment, however, a couple continues to bond. The healthy flow of oxytocin gives them warmth that draws them closer and helps them avoid the letdown of the lower dopamine levels.

Is good sex the product of a good relationship? Yes, but it works the other way around, too: a good relationship is bolstered by good sex.

## FOUR BONDS FOR KNITTING US TOGETHER

A love relationship is a complex organism. It is neither a simple agreement for cohabitation between two people nor the presence or absence of a fleeting romantic emotion. It is not simple friendship, either. Enduring love must be based on something more powerful than any of these. However, there is no single key to keeping our love strong over time.

We must build a powerful attachment, an invisible "glue," that will hold a relationship together when forces from either the outside or the inside threaten to tear it apart. We are busy, we are stressed, our hearts are restless.

*We must build a powerful attachment, an invisible "glue," that will hold a relationship together when forces from either the outside or the inside threaten to tear it apart.*

What kind of bonding agents will secure us together so strongly that none of those forces will destroy our relationship?

This adhesive is mixed from four basic ingredients. Think of them as the four bonds of love attachment. Let us look at them one by one.

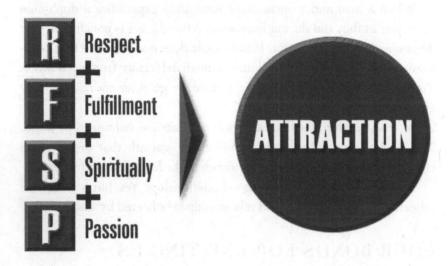

## First Bond: Respect

While we hear a great deal about the importance of communication in a marriage, I personally believe that respect is even more crucial. Why is that?

Long-term relationships mean dealing with the person rather than the picture. Up-close and personal, we see every flaw in clearer detail as time moves on. Couples begin to find increasing grounds for disappointment with each other. Perhaps a wife, after giving birth three times, no longer has the trim waistline that originally attracted her husband. He feels she is letting herself go, and his respect decreases, fair or not. Meanwhile, he sits in the recliner and flips television channels while his wife bathes and dresses the kids. She gives up on nagging but loses respect for the man she married.

The problem comes when one person treats the other with disrespect. Look up *respect* in a dictionary, and you will find the meaning I use here. Respect for another means "esteeming that person as having worth or excellence." We express this positive esteem for who and what the person is in the way we speak to and act toward that person.

Disrespect, therefore, is the opposite. It is when one person speaks to or acts toward the other in a way that communicates a lack of esteem, leaving the person with a feeling that he or she is worthless.

How have I seen it demonstrated? Let me list a couple of ways I have seen recently: a husband verbally berating his wife because her opinion on a matter differed from his; a wife snidely telling everyone at the dinner table that her husband has no business acumen and if it were not for her stepping in, they would be broke. Disrespect is any action, verbal or otherwise, that causes the other to feel a lack of worth.

Once, during Marriage Helper, our weekend workshop for marriages in crisis, I got to know a husband and wife who were on the verge of divorce. Both were highly attractive and intelligent. They came to our workshop because she had fallen in love with another man and intended to divorce her husband. Though her husband wanted to make things work, it quickly became obvious that their problems began with his disrespectful treatment of her.

She spoke of occasions when she offered an opinion of some kind. His response would be to roll his eyes and say, "You don't know what you're talking about." Let her mention how she felt about something, and he responded with a declaration that she had no right to feel that way. Rather than behaving as her partner in life, he treated her as if she were his inferior. He acted as if her thoughts and feelings had no importance at all.

She put up with years of this treatment until she met a man who gave her respect. "He's not perfect. It's not that he's the man of my dreams," she said. "The real difference is that when I speak, he listens to everything I say. He might not even agree with my comments—that is not the important thing. He lets me know that he understands why I see it the way I do. Sometimes he'll explain where he differs, but he always treats me as an equal, not some moron needing correction."

During the Marriage Helper weekend, I felt that the wife and her husband were making some progress; maybe he was beginning to see that he could rescue their relationship if he treated her with respect. Unfortunately, he never got it.

On Sunday, the husband was at the workshop alone. I had to call his wife on the phone and ask her to come, as a favor to me. She said she would do that, but only for me, not for him, because I treated her with respect. In our final sessions, there was a breakthrough on her part. She changed her mind about the future: "I'm still in love with the other man. But I'm going to stay in my marriage and try to make it work—"

Her husband interrupted. "Oh, come on, you don't love him!"

She got up and walked out of the room. I told him that he had blown his last chance and that his hope was gone. "You don't grasp the principle. She simply wanted to be treated as an equal, not a child. And she's going to the man who gives her what she needs."

Let me offer you a few simple words that will make an amazing difference in your relationship: "I can see why you would feel that way." Another version: "I understand why you would think that way."

It is not a question of wrestling our conversations into agreement on every little issue. We cannot always agree, but we *can* always offer mutual respect. When we lose that, we lose each other, because we all crave respect for who we are and for what we believe.

*Even when you do not agree,* you must treat each other with respect *if you wish for your marriage to last a lifetime.*

If this is a problem for you, and you struggle in extending respect for your partner, may I suggest that you remember this: what your mate thinks or feels is just as valid as what you think or feel. Even when you do not agree, *you must treat each other with respect* if you wish for your marriage to last a lifetime. People who are treated as inferiors in learning, logic, or emotions usually take it only for so long before all that anger explodes. When it does, your marriage may be over forever.

## Second Bond: Fulfillment

Fulfillment is about meeting each other's needs. The LovePath is a journey we continue even as we carry on the wider journey of life itself. Over time, we change and our needs change. We are alternately confident and productive, doubtful and hesitant, wounded and needy, wise and resourceful. As the poet John Donne expressed it, none of us is an island complete unto ourselves. We need someone to help us, and someone for us to help.

Just as we talked earlier about attraction being body (physical), mind (intellectual), heart (emotional), and soul (spiritual), so, too, are the areas where we should concentrate on fulfilling each other. The best way to understand how to fulfill another in all those areas is to find out what he or she wants or needs in each of those areas.

*Body.* To continue to be bonded, we must be sexually fulfilling to each other. However, it is more than just having sex. It is all that goes with it. The condition of the body. The romantic lead-up. The excitement of the act. The best way for you to understand physical fulfillment is to ask each other what would be fulfilling. While you may be hesitant to try this for fear that you will be asked to do more than you wish, it's helpful and necessary to understand your mate's needs. Ask about making love, frequency, intensity, setting, actions, and the like. Ask whether your physical appearance now— size, condition, hygiene, health—is still fulfilling to your spouse. If you find that it is not, ask why. If you learn there is something that you willingly and enthusiastically can do to become more physically attractive, do it.

*Mind.* Try the same with the area of intellectual fulfillment. We are intellectually attracted to each other as we talk about those things that are important to us. That need for conversation—meaningful dialogue—continues for the rest of our lives together. While lovers are comfortable sitting beside each other, not saying a word, they also have a need throughout life for verbal or written interaction with each other. So ask about conversation.

"Do we talk enough?"

"Do we talk about things that interest both of us?"

"Is there something more you wish from me as we talk?"

In the same vein, you may ask about intellectual stimulation. "Are we doing things that keep us growing? That keep our minds sharp? That keep us developing together as humans reaching the higher levels of life?"

Maybe one question could be this simple: "What can we do together to stimulate each of us intellectually?" If you learn there is a need or want in the intellectual realm that is not being fulfilled, talk together about how it may be fulfilled.

*Heart.* Emotional needs, of course, are paramount. In courtship we are so sensitive to one another. We have seen how, in limerence, we have an elevated level of empathy, which means we feel what our beloved feels. But what about later? Will we continue to be caring, to listen, to share burdens and pain? Unfortunately, some couples develop a degree of insensitivity to each other over time. There is no loneliness deeper than that of someone who is emotionally lonely. We need someone to hear our deepest thoughts, to tell us it's okay to feel the way we feel. We want our partner to keep saying, "I love you," on a regular basis because those words soothe and strengthen us. Not one of us is without our own unique emotional needs, and attachment deepens between us as we help each other.

Try this exercise. Every day, each of you spend ten to fifteen minutes talking about nothing but emotions and feelings. The other listens and then, in his or her own words, explains his or her understanding of those emotions. Vary the topics from day to day but stay with explaining the way you feel. Talk about children, in-laws, finances, hobbies, church, or whatever interests you. Learn to understand each other's emotions and to validate them, even if you wish that the other did not feel that way. Remember, emotions are always true for the person who has them. Denying that person the reality of those emotions demonstrates disrespect. Understanding and accepting them conveys the greatest respect anyone could ever give. It bonds you in heart as well as mind and body.

*Soul.* Fulfillment goes beyond physical, mental, and emotional needs. It goes to the very core of our existence. Whether you are religious or not, you likely feel there is some inner need that cannot be summed up in any word other than *soul* or *spirit*. It is a part of you that exists beyond the mind, heart, and body. It is the essence of who you are. This part of you needs fulfillment just as much as the other parts. It is so important that we put it into its own separate category, one of the four bonds that make a marriage great.

We will get to that next.

So, the underlying concept of fulfillment, which we will explore in our final chapters, is that through a love relationship we make each other better every week, every month, and every year. We become people we likely never would be without the encouragement and nurture that we provide each other. Fulfillment means we continue to walk the LovePath in an ascending stairway that leads to heaven itself, bringing us to higher levels of unconditional love, more meaningful lives, and more satisfying development of our gifts and talents.

Rather than letting our relationship grow stale or even die, we let it bring out our best, so that together we spiral into new and deeper forms of attraction, acceptance, and attachment. There is no limit to the heights of joy we can experience together, no boundary to our mutual fulfillment. The LovePath circles back and continues to climb.

## Third Bond: Spirituality

Are you a spiritual person?

I will answer that one for you: YES. If you are a member of the human race, it is a fact. Even if you are not religious, you are spiritual because we are all designed to be.

*If you are a member of the human race, you are spiritual.*

We live in a time when there is a renewed sense of spirituality within our culture, though it expresses itself in many forms. While I am a dedicated Christian, I want to handle this discussion in a more general way for all our readers, whether they are religious or not.

We all are creatures not only of flesh but also of spirit. We all have our thoughts about the meaning of this life, our purpose here, and the question of what may lie beyond death. Times come when we face the passing of a friend, or perhaps a troubling medical report, and we begin to think about what lies beyond our current knowledge and experience. All these are matters of the spirit, the part of us that is beyond body, mind, and heart—a part we know exists but cannot easily access. That spiritual part of us craves fulfillment just as much as the rest of us.

Is it your lover's job to fulfill you spiritually? Well, in the truest sense of the word, it is not *any*one's job to fulfill you in any way. In the purest form, fulfillment comes from within. However, when we are married, when we have a strong commitment to our lover, and when we wish for the strongest possible bond—a communion beyond the mundane—we turn to our lover for satisfaction of our physical, intellectual, emotional, and, yes, spiritual (PIES) desires.

Spiritual fulfillment comes from shared beliefs and values, shared purpose, and shared meaning. Because my wife, Alice, and I are Christians, we find this in our relationship with Jesus, which we incorporate into our relationship. Our faith is a vital part of our experience together. Perhaps yours is as well. If not, there are still ways to approach the spiritual dimension of marriage.

To discover ways for you and your mate to become spiritually fulfilling to each other, you must dig deeper than body, mind, and heart. Talk about the deepest questions of life.

"Why are we here?"

"What are we supposed to be or do?"

"What common beliefs and values do we have that sustain us in times of trouble or despair?"

These conversations lead to deeper understanding of what each partner needs. You may discover that your spouse would find a spiritual fulfillment if you went to church together, prayed together, or learned about God together. Alternatively, you may find that discussing those deeper questions of life, death, and beyond ignites the beginning of your spiritual journey together.

Houses of faith (churches, temples, fellowships, etc.) offer a wonderful environment for us to be nourished by friendships with other couples as we seek answers and reach out to God. If that is what you seek, it is important to find a house of faith where both of you feel comfortable and compelled by the activities.

Successful couples often pray, study, reflect, or meditate together. They inspire one another. To grow deeper and better attached as couples, we need to grow spiritually together.

## Fourth Bond: Passion

Our final area of attachment is the area we often associate with sexuality and, indeed, that is a part of it. However, passion is more than sex.

In the beginning of a relationship, passion often abounds. However, as we all know, time moves on. We become accustomed to each other and the newness wears off.

Is it possible to stoke the old fires of passion? Well, yes and no. Passion is stoked by fear of loss and by exploration of things new. If your marriage is healthy, you probably are not worried about losing each other. If you have made love to each other for years, there is not a lot left to explore that is new about the other's body. Some increase in passion may occur if new activities, locales, or lead-ups are added to the sexual repertoire. Of course, you can have better and more fulfilling sex, but do not count on being a perpetual teenager full of raging hormones and looking for love.

There is actually something better than that.

(One note: If you are worried that your sex life is not as it once was and you find yourself wanting more passion, then you certainly can work on your sexual relationship. I do not have the space in this book to give detailed information about how to have a wonderful sex life in your marriage, but that is precisely the focus of my PhD work. Rather than frustrating you by sharing only limited information here, I suggest you check my earlier book, *Becoming One,* for more specifics about the sexual aspects of love.)

> *The good news is that passion does not necessarily mean intense lovemaking.*

The good news is that passion does not necessarily mean intense lovemaking. At its core, passion is not about titillation or orgasms. It is about oneness. Passion that lasts a lifetime, that continues to grow no matter how old we are or how much vitality we have or what is going on in the world around us, is that of two who crave being one.

You've felt that kind of passion if you've ever experienced something wonderful—maybe a stroll in a lovely park—and found yourself wishing your spouse was there to share it with you. Shortly before I wrote this paragraph, my wonderful son-in-law, Lee Wilson, traveled with me to Alaska. Lee was wise enough to marry my daughter Joanna a few years back and provide Alice and me with two completely-doted-on grandsons. During our time in the far north, we saw several breathtaking and beautiful sites as we took side excursions from my speaking engagement.

As we drove back from one of those amazing vistas, Lee said, "I love this, but every time I see something, the first thing I feel is that I wish Joanna were here to experience it with me." *That* is passion. It is a sharing of lives; a sharing of body, mind, heart, and soul; and a sharing of dreams. It takes intentionality to devote ourselves to each other, but when we do so, we find a love deeper every day than it was the day before.

Be intentional together. Schedule time to spend with your spouse, to devote yourself to him or her, and to allow no person or thing to come before your relationship with each other. Work on that, as well as your lovemaking, and you will experience a passion more about calmness than about intensity. A passion that, in the long run, is much more fulfilling.

## YOUR ATTACHMENT

Let's pull together what we've learned in this chapter. First, if you are in a relationship, how would you describe the levels of attachment that you feel? Where are you in terms of each of the four bonds of love attachment? Which is most important to you? Which is least important?

Next, think about your level of commitment. Are you committed to this relationship because you want to be, you ought to be, or you have to be? (Hint: the best answer includes all three.) Ask yourself how strong your "want to" is and evaluate that. Then move to the "ought to," meaning your sense of obligation to your marriage, your spouse, your children, your vows, and even your religious beliefs. Evaluate how strong your commitment is in these areas.

Finally, move to the "have to." This includes all that you would lose if you lost your relationship. Time, effort, history together, closeness to your children, and, yes, even your material possessions. Evaluate how strong that type of commitment is. The higher your commitment in each of these areas, the greater likelihood your marriage will last a lifetime.

What have you learned about yourself from thinking about these concepts? How can you enhance the quality of attachment in your relationship? Give it some thought, and I would recommend that you write down some of your reflections to discuss with your partner.

In the next chapter, we will look at how to be committed to each other when you have trouble understanding each other. In my live seminars, I say it this way: "I'm going to help you understand why sometimes your spouse is just so weird."

## CHAPTER SUMMARY

- The third step on the LovePath is *attachment*. The goal of love is not the short-lived thrill of intense romance, but the long-lived comfort and fulfillment of bonding with another.
- Oxytocin is the bonding chemical produced by the human brain. Cuddling, affection, and especially orgasm release oxytocin, and, therefore, cement bonding between two people.

*Four "ingredients" help bond two people together:*
- Respect—accepting the other as the person rather than the picture you want the person to be
- Fulfillment—meeting each other's needs

- Spirituality—sharing beliefs, values, purpose, and meaning
- Passion—truly becoming one with each other by enthusiastically sharing life at all levels, far beyond sex, important though it is

*Fulfillment means to fulfill each other's needs, especially:*
- Body—being physically attractive to one's spouse and fulfilling physical needs in both action and frequency of sex
- Mind—stimulating each other to think and grow, especially by sharing ideas and lives through meaningful conversation
- Heart—exposing one's own feelings and allowing the other to be honest about his or her feelings, then responding to those emotions so as to create warm, happy, and safe feelings within the other
- Soul—living consistently by your beliefs and values and helping each other continually grow in those beliefs and values

# THE DYNAMICS OF DIFFERENCE

*John and Catherine* met on a Caribbean cruise. When a single person is looking for romance, no backdrop could be more cooperative.

Each had taken notice of the other on Day One, not long after sailing. Once or twice over the evening meal, their eyes met as they checked each other out. It was a little embarrassing but also a little exciting.

Catherine made the first move. On the deck at sunrise, she attempted to appear casual as she strolled by John, pausing to get a smile and a "Good morning" from him. They struck up a conversation that continued over breakfast.

By the third day, John and Catherine were enjoying nearly every cruise activity together, laughing, getting acquainted, and sharing life experiences. They helped each other with shopping at ports of call. By the end of the ten-day vacation, it was clear that this relationship had a future, even though the two lived in towns 150 miles apart.

This was the mid-nineties, the early days of the Internet and e-mail. Correspondence flew back and forth. On weekends John would visit Catherine's town, or she would visit his, for a romantic evening dinner or a day at the park. They made every date as romantic as possible, knowing that a Caribbean cruise—its sights, food, and beauty—was a hard act to follow.

When the wedding took place, John and Catherine had known each other for only six months. So much of the depth of their understanding of each other came from the written word, in e-mails and occasional handwritten pages.

Love letters have a wonderful tradition in the history of romance, but they are not the best way for two people to encounter the true souls of each other. Neither poetic words nor candlelit dinners over the weekend, nor even lengthy picnics in the park, show anything more than who we are on our very best behavior. John and Catherine would get to know a great deal about each other only when the honeymoon—another cruise—was over and real life began.

They are both good, solid people, these two. They have never been close to divorce, and everyone knows they are likely to make a success of their marriage. However, it has been a great deal more work than either expected.

John, who is so eloquent in his writing, so inspiring in his life philosophy, is somewhat of a slob when it comes to housekeeping. He says that clutter doesn't worry him at all. He knows where things are when he needs them. He simply wonders why Catherine will not accept that side of him. After all, he thinks, that's just who he is.

Catherine, on the other hand, believes in a place for everything and everything in its place. When her best friend from high school stopped by to visit the newlyweds, the apartment was in shambles. This caused Catherine a great deal of embarrassment. John felt bad that Catherine was hurt, but didn't do much to change his habits. And so, Catherine and John became more frustrated with each other as time went on.

It is not completely a tidy/messy thing. There are many areas in which John and Catherine each realize that they did not know each other as well as they thought before the wedding. Their love is still very strong, and they are committed to working on the relationship. They just never realized that it would take so *much* work.

In the dating stage, they could hardly stand to be separated during the week. It is not that they can hardly stand to be together now, it's that they can hardly be together without tension filling the room.

Why didn't someone warn them that a relationship would take so much work? Oh, there had been two or three obligatory premarital counseling appointments before the wedding. The pastor led these sessions, but they were perfunctory—a few general questions such as these: How did you get to know each other? Do you envision having children, and how many? Will we see you regularly here at church on Sundays?

*Why didn't someone warn them that a relationship would take so much work?*

Not a single question had prepared them for the challenge posed by actual, real-life marriage.

## TURNING ON THE LIGHT

During our weekend marriage workshops, one of our chief objectives is to help spouses understand the different approaches they take toward things. No matter how much we educate about communication, turning arguments into productive solving sessions, or compromise, couples do not "get it" until they understand their different approaches toward life. Even with all their new knowledge and skills, they still have to understand how each of them sees things differently from the other. They need to learn how to communicate in a particular manner that makes it easier for the other to digest.

Though there are many instruments available to help couples understand each other's differences, we have found that adapting one first used by Hippocrates in 300 BC is simple and effective. Of course, we don't work from his original premise that behavior is affected by body fluids, but he was very insightful in making a template that allows us a quick understanding of how to interact with another.

On the next page, we have placed a simple, four-quadrant model. Nothing unusual about that. Everybody has some kind of four-quadrant model, it seems. However, keep in mind that ours is designed to be simple and still effective. Though any number of behaviors can be used as an axis, we use these two: *processes* and *approachability*. Some people process things carefully before they act, others act before doing much processing. Some people are warm, friendly, and easy to get to know; others are cool, distant, and standoffish. Therefore, on our model we divide people as follows:

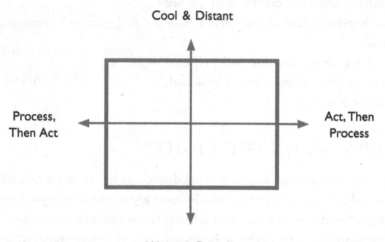

Cool & Distant

Process, Then Act

Act, Then Process

Warm & Friendly

By observing how quickly a person acts and how openly friendly he is, you can get an idea of the quadrant in which he operates. For example, a person who is cool and distant and who tends to act rapidly without much processing fits into the upper-right quadrant. Similarly, a person who is warm and friendly and tends to process before acting fits into the lower-left quadrant.

When I first meet a person, I tend to look for these two things in our initial conversations: Does she act rapidly, or does she act more slowly and thoughtfully? Is she warm and friendly, or is she cool and a little standoffish?

If she answers quickly when I ask a question, maybe even running over my talking, I see her as a *fast actor* rather than a *processor*. If she deliberates, thinks, and answers more slowly, I see her as a *slower actor* because she processes. I don't make these determinations based on one sentence or two, but after our entire conversation.

At the same time that I assess acting speed versus processing, I also assess whether she is open, immediately friendly, warm, and easy to talk with or if she is more guarded, less transparent, and a little wary. To state it more simply, I am thinking, is she fast or slow, warm or cool? From my initial impression, I assign the person a quadrant and then watch for further signs to confirm that assignment.

Sound complicated? It really is not.

The easiest way to make it clearer is to share with you the names I have assigned to each quadrant and then to explain more about people in each quadrant. After I describe all four quadrants, I will begin explaining how this works in marriage.

The chart below shows the names:

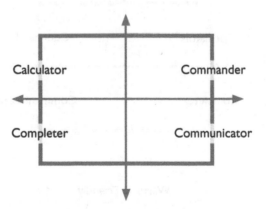

Before I begin my descriptions, be aware that a person seldom is just one of the above temperaments. Nearly all of us are combinations of two and may be a combination of three. Beyond that, everyone has a little of each quadrant. We look for prominent characteristics, not minor ones, when determining quadrant assignments.

For example, I am a *communicator-commander*. At any moment, you may see the characteristics of either temperament in my behavior. However, as with most people, circumstances and environment generally bring one to a higher level of intensity than the other. Though you haven't yet learned what each characteristic is, I will tell you that when I'm happy I'm more of a *communicator* and when I'm stressed I'm more of a *commander*.

As you read the descriptions, you may find that you, too, are more one temperament in one situation and more another temperament in a different situation. That is okay. We are not using this system to pigeonhole anyone or to make any stereotype. All of us are unique, though in ways all of us are similar. It is the similarity we use to explain the four quadrants.

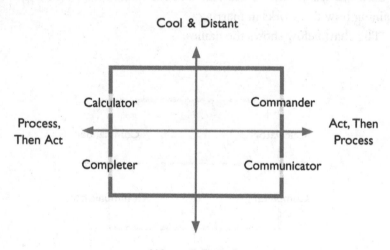

THE FAB FOUR

## Commanders

Commanders, as you can see from the model, are faster-paced actors rather than slower-paced processors. They are also cool and distant rather than warm and friendly. (They are warm and friendly in the right situations with the right people. However, we are assessing usual behavior rather than occasional behavior.) Commanders are bottom-line, make-it-happen people. They are driving, demanding, and assertive. They tend to take charge of a situation and lead. They tend to focus more on results than the process to get the results.

Commanders can be direct, assertive, demanding, and strong willed. They are likely to step on a few toes at times. Sometimes others consider them rude, though commanders do not think themselves rude at all, just as people who say things plainly. They are driven individuals, ambitious and goal oriented.

*Commanders are bottom-line, make-it-happen people. They are driving, demanding, and assertive.*

They are also impulsive. They do not want to be burdened with too many details or too much talk when a decision needs to be made. They are competitive. They tend to be strong personalities with strong egos.

Commanders are not show-offs in the usual sense of the word, but they do like to be noticed. They may be namedroppers, may surround themselves with items that show they are successful or powerful, and may display quite a bit of self-confidence, even if they do not really feel it at a given moment.

If they face a problem, their solution is likely to be quick and harsh. They are quick to anger.

The flip side of that anger is they also tend to get over things quickly. For them life is a series of events that are not necessarily connected. They may be in an argument one moment, reach an acceptable conclusion, and then take the person they were arguing with to lunch without any remorse or recrimination. Once it is over, it is over. (However, if they feel that they lost and that the other person had some unfair advantage, they will not move on so easily. They do not like being taken advantage of.)

If you think you or your spouse may be a commander, but not

every description given above fits, remember what I wrote earlier: most people have a combination of temperaments rather than only one. Everything said above may be moderated by also having some of the characteristics of other temperaments.

## Calculators

As you see from the model, calculators are slower-paced processors rather than faster-paced actors. They tend to be cool and distant, keeping their emotions to themselves (though they may be warm and friendly in certain situations). They are analytical, detail driven, and unhappy with shoddy work. Rather than focusing on results, as do commanders, they focus on whether the results were achieved *correctly*. The process is extremely important to them, and even if good results come about, they are unhappy if the process was flawed or abandoned in achieving those results. Being right is crucial, and if they are wrong, it is personal and bothers them greatly.

They do not just play by the rules; they have the rulebook memorized. While someone else may be ready to move into action, the calculator wants to process all the facts, do all the research, and get every duck in a row before proceeding. Actually, that is how they handle problems—analyzing and processing before taking any action.

*Calculators do not just play by the rules; they have the rulebook memorized.*

They are careful, cautious, tidy people. Everything has a place and is in it.

They tend to be possessive of space and items. Slide over to their side of the bed and you are likely to be told where each person's private space is on that bed. They do not want you to use their things or get into their personal space. If you get physically too close to calculators, they will either move themselves or move you.

Calculators tend to have trouble understanding emotional people. They themselves primarily get emotional only if the rules are not being followed or if they were proven wrong when they were convinced of their rightness. Therefore, they have trouble understanding why some people feel as intently as they do about life. If you are hurting, they will do all they can to help, but do not expect them to know the right words to say or to understand all that you are going through. They are not heartless; they just can't relate what you are feeling to their own experiences.

## Completers

Completers are slower-paced processors who are also warm and friendly. They are wonderful people who care deeply about family, tradition, and loyalty. They are deliberate, methodical, and habitual, but they are adaptable when they need to be. They dislike conflict, and one of the ways they handle problems is simply to avoid the problem as long as they can. Though amiable people, they tend not to be very emotional, having more of an even keel when sailing through life.

> *Completers are wonderful people who care deeply about family, tradition, and loyalty.*

People tend to like completers because they are usually great listeners. Completers may hear more about others' struggles with life than any of the rest of the temperaments, because people tend to trust them. They are viewed as mature, stable, and trustworthy.

Completers tend to be laid back and are unhurried by time pressures. Though they typically do not process as long or deeply as calculators, they do process before acting and will think things through as carefully as they can. They may seek advice or simply test what others are thinking before making a decision. However, do not let their laid-back approach lead you to think that they are weak willed or easy to convince. They will smile, nod their heads, and listen so that you may think you have won them over to your way of thinking, only to discover that they were being polite but have quite a strong and different perspective than the one you shared with them.

Because they are so nice, polite, and kind, some may think that completers are to be ignored. However, that would be a mistake. Not only do they do the detailed work that others, such as commanders, desperately need someone to do, they often are the backbone of an organization. They can stay at the same job, doing the same thing, for as long as it takes to get it done. Beyond that, of the four temperaments, they are the ones most likely to hurt you if you attempt to hurt something they love. They are mild mannered but definitely not weak. If you wish to be attacked in full fury, threaten anything the completer loves; you will be surprised at the quick, powerful, and effective response.

Because completers are family oriented and loyal, they tend to have the most trouble overcoming hurts done to them or disloyalty shown to them. For them everything in life relates to everything else, and their memories challenge even the mythological memory of elephants. Though they can forgive, it takes time and a slow rebuilding of trust.

## Communicators

Communicators are warm and friendly and are fast-paced actors rather than slow-paced processors. They are verbal, active, and emotional. People see them as outgoing, demonstrative, enthusiastic, and inspiring. While the commander may step on a few toes, the communicator feels it when you step on his toes. He is sensitive, popularity driven, and in need of your approval. Communicators need to be liked; it bothers them terribly if they think you do not like them. Therefore, their preferred way of solving problems is to appease everyone if possible.

*Communicators can talk to anyone, anywhere, at any time, and are not intimidated by strangers or new social situations.*

Communicators love to talk and are usually quite good at it, using voice inflections and hand gestures to make their points. They can talk to anyone, anywhere, at any time, and are not intimidated by strangers or new social situations. Sometimes they will even do your talking for you, finishing your sentences or interrupting you before you are done.

Because they are so good at communicating, they tend to have charisma and personal magnetism. They are natural humorists, the life of the party, and inspiring cheerleaders who are optimistic about what we can all do if we work together. Actually, that is also the way they tend to see life, with optimism that everything will turn out okay. However, they are not always optimistic and can become emotional very quickly. As with commanders, they are impulsive, but their impulsiveness is more likely to do something fun—or appeasing to others—whereas the commander's impulsiveness is more likely to result in some quick move to achieve victory.

If you notice, communicators are exactly diametrical to calculators, just as commanders are to completers. Diametrical positions on the chart tend to indicate great differences. For example, calculators are neat, tidy, and disciplined; communicators, generally speaking, are not so inclined. They tend to have clutter around them, either at home, at work, or in their automobile. They also tend to lose things because of their lack of attention to detail and may spend a great deal of time looking for misplaced keys and the like.

Communicators are fun people to be with, but if they are not comfortable with you, they will find a way to get away from you. They prefer being with people they like and who they feel like them.

## What About You?

If you find yourself wondering which temperament, or combination of temperaments, you are, you can discover more at our website, www.MarriageHelper.com. We do online profiling for those who enroll in our couples-in-crisis weekend workshop. If you want only a better idea and not the actual profile, there is a short instrument available in the workbook that accompanies this book. While it is not as precise and thorough as the online profile, it may give you more insight into your temperament.

# THE TEMPERAMENTS ON THE LOVEPATH

While understanding your own and your spouse's temperament isn't essential to continuing on the LovePath, it sure is helpful. First, it helps to understand that it's okay to be different from each other and that neither is better than the other. Second, it helps to understand why your beloved sometimes acts in ways that are difficult for you to understand or appreciate. Third, it helps give you an understanding for interacting that makes communication much more effective than it may have been up until now.

Your differing temperaments blend you into a wonderful relationship, where each of you brings certain strengths. (For example, if one of you is the calculator or completer, you are likely the better one to handle finances because of your steadiness, thoroughness, and lack of impulsivity, especially when it comes to spending.)

But one of the areas where understanding the temperaments helps most is in communicating. When you understand each other's temperaments or combination of temperaments, you can learn to communicate in a way that the other person understands more clearly and quickly. Imagine it: no more confusion or cross-communication!

Here, then, are things to keep in mind when communicating to the specific types:

*Commanders*
- Don't give too many details.
- Be efficient.
- Don't bruise his or her ego.
- Talk about the results rather than the process.
- Let the commander know that you appreciate his or her position and authority, but don't be intimidated by it or give the impression you're not as important or strong.
- Don't challenge the commander in such a way that there will

be a winner and loser, or you will kick into gear the commander's competitive need to win.

- Be strong and confident.

*Calculators*

- Don't rush things.
- Be prepared to answer many questions.
- Have your documentation ready to help explain your point.
- Talk unemotionally and rationally.
- Allow the calculator to process for as long as it takes.
- Be sure that you do not suggest anything that may be seen as a flight of fancy or violating the rules.

*Completers*

- Be patient.
- Be calm and collected.
- Focus on what's truly important to the completer (family, tradition, and loyalty).
- Don't think that smiles and nods mean agreement.
- Be ready to listen carefully to what the completer thinks, and ask for that feedback as you progress.
- Don't press for fast decisions unless absolutely necessary.
- Keep in mind the completer's need for safety, security, and having no risk.

*Communicators*

- Be ready for the conversation to stray from time to time as the communicator gets ideas or is reminded of other matters as you talk.
- Remember to be careful in showing any kind of disapproval that the communicator may read as a rejection.
- Focus on what's truly important to the communicator (people, interactions, popularity, and being liked).

- Don't get uptight if the conversation occasionally becomes playful; gently guide it back to the topic after allowing the communicator to enjoy your company, humor, and goodwill.
- Don't let yourself chase dreams that he or she will bring up (they may sound wonderful but will actually prevent you from accomplishing what you need to accomplish). As often as not, communicators process things verbally, and these dreams aren't something they really want to do or achieve; they're just a way to explore the ideas being discussed.
- When you disagree, make it clear that you are disagreeing with the idea but that you still hold the communicator in high regard and appreciate his or her creativity.

## MIXING AND MATCHING TEMPERAMENTS

While some people marry people similar to themselves in age, religion, socioeconomic status, ethnicity, and the like, it seems that many marry a temperament or set of temperaments different from their own. One theory is that we are drawn to a person of different temperament because it tends to balance us out. Therefore, a person who is primarily a commander may marry a person who is primarily a completer, and a communicator may marry a calculator, and so on.

*When two people are in the same temperament quadrant, they tend to get along very well if they respect each other.*

With the couples, I've noted that when the two are in the same temperament quadrant, they tend to get along very well if they respect each other.

For example, I recently worked with two commanders who were on the verge of divorce. Each was strong willed and dominant in behavior. They clashed for years and were ready to call it quits rather than fight any longer. Solving their problem was relatively simple.

First, I helped them understand that because they were both

commanders, they should expect to be competitive and to disagree strongly when each felt that he or she should "win" on a particular matter. That behavior was normal to their temperaments and did not mean that either was mean, uncaring, or unloving. It simply means that they are commanders doing what commanders do.

Second, I helped them understand that strong disagreements and competitiveness are okay—maybe even interesting—if in their disagreements they were careful to demonstrate respect and understanding to the other. A commander who feels disrespected typically turns very nasty.

Third, I shared with them tools to use when they disagreed so that rather than having an argument that divided them, they could work out a compromise that would satisfy them both. As simple as those three things may sound, it worked a miracle in their relationship. It did not change who either of them was or how either one of them saw the world. It changed the way they saw and interacted with each other. That is all it took to get them to cancel the pending divorce and work out a relationship fulfilling to each.

Using that same principle, remember when you interact with your spouse to communicate in a style that is clear to his or her temperament. When talking—or disagreeing—with a commander, speak commander. Same with the calculator, completer, and communicator. Know that a commander focuses on results and likes to lead, a calculator focuses on correctness and likes to analyze, a completer focuses on security and likes to listen, and a communicator focuses on interaction with people and likes to talk. Therefore, a commander fears being taken advantage of, a calculator fears being wrong, a completer fears losing security, and a communicator fears being disliked. If you keep that in mind, then you can communicate with an understanding of why your spouse may see things differently from you, or why he or she sometimes has a different set of priorities or goals. It does not make him or her wrong, intractable, or even malicious. It simply means that you are different, and you need to honor those differences.

That means that a communicator in a relationship with a calculator should expect the calculator to sometimes feel the communicator is out of control, disorganized, or even untrustworthy. In turn, the calculators should expect the communicator to sometimes feel that the calculator is dull, stuffy, or too focused on logic.

Let me give an example.

One couple, where the husband is a calculator and the wife is a communicator, had a challenge because of her attempts to be romantic. He returned from a long business trip to find flower petals spread from the door to the bedroom, across the bedroom floor, up to the place on the bed where she reclined in exotic lingerie. His reaction? "Who made this mess? What were you thinking? Who's going to clean all this up?" Her reaction? Feelings of hurt, rejection, and that he did not love her as much as he loved neatness.

Now, think how much better that encounter would have turned out if the husband/calculator had understood the wife/communicator's need for something new and exciting and had yielded to that rather than his need for neatness and things to be in order.

Similarly, a commander married to a completer should understand that the completer will be very unhappy with risky financial ventures that the commander may see as the way to success.

Furthermore, when commanders see the need for confrontation, they do it quickly and harshly to get the matter settled. I sometimes view commanders as snapping turtles. Completers tend to avoid conflict, and when they do participate, may do it in a passive-aggressive way that frustrates the commander. I view completers as the box turtles that get halfway across the highway before becoming afraid and closing up. That means that when commanders try to force the completers into confrontation to solve a matter, the completer is likely to clam up and find a way to fight back that frustrates the commander even more because he cannot prove that she is even fighting. The commander's best bet is to approach matters of disagreement in calmer times and allow the completer the freedom to work into it slowly.

There are many combinations, and to describe them all would take another book. Hopefully, the snapshots above will give you some idea of how to communicate with each other. Try your best to speak the other's language—commander, calculator, completer, or communicator. This will help you evaluate each other's meaning or tactics based not on personal reaction but on an understanding of each other's temperaments and needs.

## TEMPERAMENTAL SEX

Before closing this chapter, I wish to share with you a few comments on how each temperament approaches lovemaking.

*Commanders* tend to have the largest egos and, therefore, want to believe that each encounter is fabulous for the partner. They may become outstanding lovers, not just because they love their mate, but also because they want to be the best at lovemaking that anyone could be. If your spouse is a commander, understand that ego and cater to it when making love. Stroke his or her ego as much as you honestly can. Whatever you do, do NOT disparage his or her body, technique, or ability. Attack a commander's ego, and he or she will be extremely hurt and may have great trouble ever getting over it. One completer wife I know decided to hurt her commander husband in one argument by telling him that his physical endowment made it impossible for him to be an adequate lover. He will never forget that, no matter how many times she apologizes and tries to explain that she did not mean it. For the rest of their lives, it will always be in his mind when they make love . . . if they make love.

*For completers, lovemaking is the natural following of a relationship that is tender, caring, and fulfilling in every other manner.*

*Calculators* approach sex the same way they approach everything else in life—by the rules. If you wish your calculator lover to act or be different in lovemaking, you will have to adequately prove that the different behavior you request is not in violation of whatever rules the calculator lives by.

*Completers* are the true romantics. Because they are so focused on home, family, and the like, lovemaking for them is an extension of that relationship in greater ways than the other temperaments. As I often tell audiences, foreplay for a completer begins over breakfast . . . yesterday. A call during the day, flowers for no reason, helping to bathe and put the kids to bed all constitute foreplay for the completer. Lovemaking is the natural following of a relationship that is tender, caring, and fulfilling in every other manner.

*Communicators* approach lovemaking the same way they do everything else in life: they want variety, excitement, and new experiences. They love pleasant surprises. They like to try the untried. At the same time, they love it when lovemaking includes verbal caresses, instructions, or exclamations of delight. Make it fun, and the communicator really enjoys lovemaking. Make it routine, and he or she will likely find it boring. If you are married to a communicator, I advise at least every few weeks to introduce some new lingerie, setting, technique, or idea. They will love you for it.

It is all in understanding what and how to communicate to your mate.

## CHAPTER SUMMARY

Though understanding the differences between you and your lover is not a step on the LovePath, it can be quite helpful in maintaining the attachment step of the LovePath.

Appreciating differences gives greater ability to demonstrate respect, to accept the other as he or she is rather than a picture he or she presents. (Remember, respect is one of the four "glues" that bonds people in attachment.)

To understand this model of human behavior, we use two criteria:

- Does the person act before processing, or process before acting?
- Is the person warm and friendly, or more cool and distant?

The most important thing to learn from this four-quadrant model of temperaments is how to communicate most effectively with the other person.

The temperamental differences between the two people will present both strengths and weaknesses to the relationship. Understanding those makes life easier and the relationship more fulfilling. Temperamental differences apply to every dimension of human behavior, including lovemaking.

# RELATIONSHIP
# IN RETREAT

*When Will and* Rita married in the mid-1950s, it was a different world.

Those were boom years, postwar years when young adults were in a hurry to build families and businesses. It was not unusual for an eighteen- or nineteen-year-old man to take a wife, to begin at the bottom of the corporate ladder, and to be a father of three or four children before he was thirty. At fifty, he might well live in the same home, have the same wife, and work in the same business (hopefully with a few promotions on his résumé). Theirs was a generation characterized by loyalty and consistency. Today Will wonders how young adults can jump from job to job and relationship to relationship. When he makes a commitment to a company or a home, by golly he stands by it, no matter how much pain he must hold inside to do it.

Will and Rita started dating in high school. They knew each other since tenth grade and had a few dates in the eleventh grade, but things were not too serious at that young age. Will grew up idolizing his big brother who fought at Okinawa, and he knew that he would be signing up for the army the day after his high school graduation.

After one tour in Korea, Will was back in the States. He was ready to find a mate, settle down, and enjoy a job and a family. Rita was still in the phone book, still single, still shyly interested in him. It was not long before the couple was married and occupying a small ranch-style house. Will had a sales job in industrial equipment—small pay, promising future.

The first few years of marriage were all about work and raising children. There simply was not a great deal of time for Will and Rita to ponder the intimacy of their marriage. However, children have a way of growing up much more rapidly than we expect or even desire. The time came when all but one of the kids were beginning their own adult journeys. Will and Rita found that their home had suddenly fallen silent, and they were not sure what to say to each other.

For years there had been the occasional unpleasant exchange, usually stifled so as not to upset the children. Rita thought Will was distant and uncommunicative. He seemed more interested in football, basketball, or whatever other sport was on television than in the things she needed to tell him. Will thought Rita expected too much of him. Didn't he work fifty hours a week so that she could stay home, run his household, and raise his children?

In time it simply became easier to tread softly around each other. In the new house that came after Will's second promotion and their third child, Rita had her own sewing room with her own television. She spent evenings there running the sewing machine, watching her detective shows, and leaving her husband to do his own thing. After a few years, a twin bed appeared in the sewing room and Rita slept in it.

Will would not admit his hurt over what seemed like Rita's abandonment. Anyone who came to the house could see that there were separate living arrangements, and this offended his male pride. Nevertheless, he had no idea what to do or say about it. He was a salesman and he could engage any new client and talk his way to a sales offer. Yet somehow over the years of hurry and scurry, he had forgotten how to sit down and talk with his own wife. When they were together, the air seemed to be thick with issues and emotions that did not quite fit into words. Will and Rita felt as if they stood on two separate islands that were drifting apart, and there was no way the two worlds could ever be joined together again.

Will realized that he had no idea who Rita was anymore. Once, years ago, they had sat on the back porch every evening and talked casually about their day. In the early years, during the week, he would call her on the phone just to hear her voice. Now he knew almost nothing about her world. She knew almost nothing about his. Even worse, as far as he could tell, she was not even curious.

When Will and Rita were in their late forties, after a miserable Christmas together, there was a single tentative discussion about divorce. At that point, the disagreements were a little angrier. Yet neither of them quite had the heart to leave. The cost, in so many ways, would simply be too great.

The cost of not leaving, on the other hand, was an indefinite future of living in the same home as strangers who had forgotten how to be lovers. Work associates asked him questions about his wife, and he was embarrassed in his inability to provide any answers. Will realized it was possible to live the rest of his life in a kind of standoff, a mutually assured misery.

That was their life for several years afterward, as the anger cooled by increasing emotional distance that could end only in apathy.

## A TWO-WAY STREET

Have you ever been a visitor in an unfamiliar city? You drive along, searching for some destination, checking street names and landmarks. After a turn or two, you suddenly find that some of the scenery is oddly familiar. Have you ever been here before? Yes, you have, twenty minutes ago and from the opposite direction. You are heading down the same boulevard, going the other way.

The LovePath can be much like that. At its beginning, we find *attraction*, which is about drawing closer. We move forward along the path and pass through the region of *acceptance*, which is about coming to care. Then there is that long stretch we call *attachment*, when, if things go well, we grow wiser as partners, deeper in intimacy, better at giving, and more joyful in receiving.

In truth the road divides into two paths. However, we are so engrossed in the journey by that time that we often do not realize whether we are stagnating, taking one road, the other one, or even moving back down the path in reverse.

> *If things go well in attachment, we grow wiser as partners, deeper in intimacy, better at giving, and more joyful in receiving.*

From attachment there are two primary ways forward on the LovePath. We might call them the *upward spiral* and the *downward spiral*.

## The Upward Spiral

This is the direction true and mature love takes. It is, as it sounds, a spiral upward to the zenith of a relationship, a path toward love that becomes ever more satisfying as we grow together. What is happening is that we are once again cycling through higher stages of attraction, acceptance, and attachment, each cycle more fulfilling than the ones that came before because of an added dimension.

The name for this upward spiral is *aspiration*, because to aspire means to aim, to seek ambitiously, to soar, or to desire something of great value. The original root word means "breathing" or "panting in pursuit of something." As the LovePath leads us onward, spiraling up the skyward path, we feel a second wind. Our strength is renewed, and the upward spiral takes us to heights where the air is cool and the view is magnificent.

## The Downward Spiral

Those who go in this direction in their relationship typically do not intend to choose that path—no one ever intends to bring about their own unhappiness—but it happens with the accumulation of smaller choices that are unhealthy and unloving. The path of aspiration teaches us to give, to honor, to respect, and to enjoy those things. This downward path is the opposite. It is taking, dishonoring, disrespecting, controlling, and dominating a partner. One direction is about freedom and the other leads to bondage.

Later in the book, we will consider each of these two remarkably opposite destinations.

## Stagnation

Sometimes people do not move at all, but simply stagnate at attachment and never progress, regress, or anything else. They are attached to each other for life and seem not to care significantly if they grow closer than they were the day they married. However, this condition is extremely rare in my experience working with couples. Very few can simply stop at a point on the LovePath and remain there for years. Typically, they move either forward or backward.

That leads me to the fourth way, which is the path of turning around and going back down the LovePath.

## The LovePath U-turn

Yes, it is possible to return down the path in the direction from which we came. This begins when our attachments begin to weaken rather than strengthen. Perhaps respect diminishes. Maybe there is less fulfillment. Passion dies. There could be a diminished attention to growing together spiritually. Whatever the cause, the mutual commitment to each other begins to lessen. As attachment is slowly undone, acceptance, too, will move in the wrong direction. Finally, two people find that they are no longer attracted to each other. In other words, the path has been traveled backward. The act of backtracking on the LovePath is known as *apathy*.

How many people do you believe walk this direction?

Untold millions.

Let us learn how it happens.

## DRIFTING APART

It happens so often: two partners start out as a perfect fit but drift apart until a great emotional distance separates them. How can a once beautiful and passionate love grow so cold and so miserable?

It happens gradually, often almost imperceptibly at the outset, and then gains speed. The attachment stage is about commitment. Part of that commitment is to fulfill each other, but for any number of reasons many couples lose that fulfillment over time. Typically when one person begins to feel a lack of fulfillment, he or she will tell the other. However, most of the time, the unfulfilling partner either does not hear it or ignores the importance of it. For example, if a husband tells his wife that he is no longer sexually satisfied—he may say it crudely rather than eloquently—the all-too-typical response of the wife is to explain to him reasons why she isn't satisfying him. "We're not twenty any longer. We both work. The children wear me out."

Though she means those words to serve both as an explanation and as a shield from having to do anything more sexually than she already does, he hears a very different message: "I know you think you need that, but you don't!" No matter how much she explains why she is not doing it or cannot do it, if it is a need he has, he will not be satisfied as long as that need is unfulfilled. Her reasons seem no more than excuses to him, and he moves slightly away from her because of his frustration. They are already in trouble but he is the only one who knows it—and yet even he does not yet know just how much trouble they actually are in.

Name the need and change the story above to fit that need. The principle works whether the need is sexual fulfillment, meaningful conversations, more affection, or living safely and securely within financial boundaries. No matter which spouse, no matter what need, if one is unfulfilled and the other does not respond to the cry for fulfillment, the unfulfilled spouse begins moving away. Does that mean the marriage is doomed? Not yet. However, if the pattern continues, it will not be long until there are serious problems in the acceptance stage.

You recall that in acceptance we feel loved for the person we are rather than the picture we project. We know that our beloved sees our faults, knows our history, understands our desires, and still loves us. Unfortunately, when we feel that our lover no longer cares enough to fulfill our needs, we also feel that our lover no longer truly understands us at all and certainly does not accept us as we are. The trip back down the path gets a little faster, goes a little further. The marriage is not over, but it definitely is not where it once was. We stay together but the intensity of commitment and the feelings of deep, abiding love wane. We tend to become roommates who may or may not have sex occasionally, but the person that used to be the love of our life no longer is our focus.

*If one is unfulfilled and the other does not respond to the cry for fulfillment, the unfulfilled spouse begins moving away.*

We have drifted apart, and the distance is slowly widening.

When this distance occurs, if any negative behavior becomes part of the relationship, it is far less likely that the offended party will stand beside or rescue the offender. For example, he may have helped her through a struggle with alcohol before, when they were committed and close, but now he may see her bottle as a sign that the relationship should end. Or she may have been patient and understanding in helping him overcome his porn addiction when they were in full attachment, but because of where she has retreated to on the LovePath, she washes her hands in disgust and walks away from the marriage when he continues his addiction.

When we are unfulfilled, ultimately what we feel most prominently is the sting of rejection. We only know that that wonderful feeling of being accepted for who we are, for the real person that we continue to be, has been lost, and we resent our partner for withdrawing the love that before was freely given. The more we think about it, the more we find other things to resent about that partner—things that did not bother us at all in the past. Finally, we no longer feel attracted to the person who once overwhelmingly attracted us. None of the attractions (remember the acronym PIES: *physical, intellectual, emotional,* and *spiritual*) affect us as profoundly as they once did. Eventually, we stop liking anything about the person who was once the love of our life.

Did you follow the progression—or rather, the regression—in the person who is moving away? Attachment weakens and becomes detachment. Acceptance fades, changing to rejection. Ultimately, attractiveness deteriorates to the point that rather than being drawn to the person, we are repelled.

## A Warning About Attraction

Though acceptance is the key to true love, as we have discussed in detail, attraction is also extremely important throughout a relationship. Just as each of the four bonds of attraction, the PIES, has a positive effect in drawing two people closer, they can with time move from positive to neutral, no longer drawing them together. Even worse, they can become negative, repelling at least one from the other.

For example, a woman may be attracted to a man emotionally. He makes her feel special. He makes her laugh. He fulfills her needs to feel appreciated, to feel important, and to have a special place in his life. However, with time, especially if they have been together for a while, he may no longer do the things that evoke those positive emotions within her. His funny sayings and actions seem to be reserved for others. He pays little attention to her, demonstrates little affection, and generally ignores her except when he needs food or sex. Therefore, his emotional attractiveness that existed in the beginning gradually fades to neutral. She does not find him emotionally attractive any longer. She also does not necessarily find him unattractive. From her viewpoint they drift into a relationship that is neither great nor terrible.

If he continues to ignore her, he may eventually become emotionally repulsive to her. If she wants to feel positive emotions when she is with him, she may resent his lack of attention to such a degree that she feels negative emotions just being near him.

As happens too often, he may evolve into ways of interacting with her that cannot lead to anything but negative feelings toward him. If he treats her badly—with criticism, contempt, abuse, lying, mockery, embarrassment—then his actions evoke bad emotions: shame, anger, hurt, resentment, bitterness. Soon the very thought of him makes her want to be free from him. More than unattractive, he is repulsive.

Just as attraction draws one closer, repulsion pushes one further away.

This next example may tread on dangerous ground, but it needs to be said.

In my work with marriages, I find many men who were physically attracted to their wives when they courted. That physical attraction continued in their early years together. However, with time she let herself go. (This is not about the normal effects of aging. Rather, we're referring to body changes from bad habits.) Many men tell me that they love their wife as much as they ever did, but they no longer find her physically attractive. Because of changes in her physically, she moved into neutral territory, and finally, as she continued to gain weight, into the negative. One man said, "If it were something she couldn't help, I'd have no problem. But this isn't a disease, it's a lack of caring about what's important to me. She doesn't have to be this heavy, but she likes her food more than she cares about my being drawn to her body." It can just as easily be the man who becomes physically unattractive, whether through weight gain or, as one wife said, "He reeks of tobacco. I can't stand to smell him."

Please don't think I am suggesting that we should meet Hollywood or Madison Avenue expectations of beauty. My point is that both men and women should recognize that the attraction steps along the Love-Path are important for a lifetime. Moving into neutral may not be ultra-damaging. However, moving into negative always causes problems. If we are to maintain our growth on the LovePath, we must always care enough to be as attractive as we can be at our age and situation in life.

Additionally, just as a person may become unattractive physically or emotionally, that may also occur intellectually (one keeps growing, the other doesn't) and spiritually (one deepens and the other does not).

*If we are to maintain our growth on the LovePath, we must always care enough to be as attractive as we can be at our age and situation in life.*

The primary point in this section is that the more unattached, unaccepted, and unattracted we feel, the more we pull back and backtrack down the LovePath. We begin to put up barriers so that we will not feel the lack of fulfillment so acutely. We find refuge in other things. In the case of Will, it was initially TV sports; for his wife, it was a room of her own, where she wouldn't face the awkward silence that occurred when her husband was around.

One day a more significant barrier formed itself.

## TWO'S COMPANY, THREE'S A CROWD

Neither Will nor Rita had intended to move away from each other, but it happened all the same. When Rita eventually moved a bed into her sewing room, Will was hurt, though he understood well enough that he had contributed to the distance between his wife and himself. The backtracking path from mutual attachment becomes a journey back to independence. Will was not quite sure what to do with his share of it.

He often stopped at a coffee shop on Monday mornings before leaving for his weekly sales calls. Over time Will developed a casual, conversational friendship with a waitress named Jeanette. As he grew lonelier and more distanced from his wife, he found himself having longer chats with the young lady. He was flattered that she seemed so attentive, but he refused to think that there was anything there but a common friendship. Therefore, he put no emotional barriers in place; he allowed himself to be drawn to Jeanette. If he was not traveling, he began to stop by the coffee shop more frequently, for lunch or a snack. Then he found himself frequenting the shop during times when he knew that customers would be few, and Jeanette would be free to converse without interruptions.

There was certainly an attraction, though Will hardly considered it anything but innocent. As he and Jeanette got to know each other better, the attraction moved to acceptance. They began to care beyond the level of friendship. Will was developing a strong liking for someone else's attentions, and, therefore, the process of detachment from Rita, his own wife, accelerated.

Will finally realized he was infatuated with a young woman who was not his wife. This shocked him—and then it excited him. Yes, he was in love with Jeanette. Why not? She listened to him. She cared about the same things he did. Why, she knew more about his life these days than the stranger in the sewing room! Jeanette was fun and physically attractive, as well as intellectually and emotionally attractive. He could not see a flaw in her.

**Attraction to Another** > **Acceptance Develops** > **Attachment Becomes Powerful**

Meanwhile, what were his thoughts about Rita? Oh, he still loved her—like a sister. Rita was a good person, and he would always care for her. But for now, all he could think about was Jeanette.

Yes, you know the script by now: limerence is powerful. An unhappily married individual is at high risk to be struck by its sledgehammer of emotions. The dopamine flow is a lot more enjoyable than common depression. The drop in serotonin levels nudges the infatuated person to do things he might not do otherwise, such as bed down one night at a girl's apartment. That is what Will did with Jeanette. Even though Rita was sleeping in a separate room back home, she could surmise what was going on. Spouses often seem to have a kind of sixth sense about being betrayed.

Will's stimulated mind found more and more reasons that he should be with the coffee-shop waitress instead of his wife. Human nature helped him rationalize his actions, so it seemed to him that it was all Rita's fault anyway, and that loving Jeanette felt so good that it could not be wrong. Will was a religious person, by the way. He had attended church all his life and knew all the Christian teachings about faithfulness and the sanctity of marriage. So powerful were his feelings, however, that he managed not to think about those years of teachings. God must have sent him Jeanette, he thought instead. "God will work it out for all three of us, and everyone will live happily ever after."

*Spouses often seem to have a kind of sixth sense about being betrayed.*

If anyone had been around to tell Will that it never works out that way, he would not have believed it.

Will loved two women at the same time: he had a sibling love for his wife and an erotic, emotional love for Jeanette. Such situations cannot last, of course. One will expand to push out the other. Either Will's marriage would be rescued by the love, patience, and perseverance of his wife or he would leave his marriage to devote himself to his new love.

# THE OTHER AFFAIRS

Dr. Willard Harley, author of several books including the bestseller *His Needs, Her Needs,* once told me over dinner that 60 percent of all marriages are affected by an extramarital affair at some time during the marriage. I responded that I did not have any empirical evidence on that subject, but that my experience working with thousands of couples led me to believe he was right.

However, if you expand the concept of what an affair is, the statistics are much worse.

There are less obvious ways for us to be unfaithful than by committing adultery. The principles are the same whether we are talking about a man or a woman who becomes the third party in a marriage or whether it is something else entirely. There are the same patterns of decreasing dependence in the marriage, emotional transfer to someone or something else, and the final crisis of making the decision either to rescue the marriage or to abandon it for the looming alternative.

*There are less obvious ways for us to be unfaithful than by committing adultery.*

Here are a few nonsexual affairs I have seen become the dividing point in a marriage:

- *Alcohol, food, or drugs.* One spouse becomes so addicted to a method of self-medication that he or she will not stop, even at the cost of the marriage.
- *Work.* Some sublimate the love and commitment they once had for a spouse into the pursuit of a career. Desires for money, power, and prestige feed into this temptation, and it becomes an ever-present refuge when we are frustrated with our personal relationships. Some men and women begin bringing attaché cases and laptop computers home not because they need to work, but because they either no longer

remember how to interact with their family or simply no longer want to.

- *Family of origin.* Some people never allow themselves to reach the level of absolute attachment and commitment of true love because they do not allow their lover to become the most important person in their lives. Instead their attachment to their parents, brothers, or sisters makes them so controlled by their original family that their lovers never take their rightful places in their hearts.

- *Hobbies.* There are men who disappear into the woods to hunt and fish every weekend for long wild-game seasons, or perhaps they live on the golf course. There are women who are involved in clubs or church events to such an excessive extent that they are never at home. Some people become so emotionally attached to computers, e-mail, online chat rooms, and Internet surfing that they all but disappear into the circuitry. Whatever it is, anything that keeps a man and woman from growing in love for each other is an unwanted "lover" taking away the time, focus, and attention a spouse deserves.

- *Friendship.* Could a thing as good as a friendship break up a marriage? I have seen it happen. I know a woman who became so thoroughly involved—nonsexually—with a female friend that she finally left her husband. She believed that her friendship was more fulfilling and emotionally valuable than her marriage.

I could make a list so long that it would take another book or two to complete it, but you get the idea. Think of it this way: adultery is the violation of the marriage contract that occurs when the spouse is supplanted by someone or something else. Theologians might not define it that way, but those of us who work with thousands of couples each year know that it is true.

# HOW TO KNOW WHEN YOU'VE CROSSED THE BOUNDARIES

If you or your spouse wonders whether a relationship with another person has gone too far—or whether a person might be having an "affair" with work, alcohol, or anything else—there is a simple way to get a good idea.

## *CAGE*

To get a picture of whether you, or your spouse, may have crossed a boundary, allow me to show you how you can use a modification of a tool used to assess potential alcoholics. It was developed by Dr. John Ewing, founding director of the Bowles Center for Alcohol Studies at the University of North Carolina at Chapel Hill. When working with potential alcoholics, many primary care physicians use Dr. Ewing's CAGE questionnaire to determine the likelihood of alcoholism. It is very effective and used internationally with great success.

The questionnaire goes like this:

C—Have you ever felt you should Cut down on your drinking?
A—Have people Annoyed you by criticizing your drinking?
G—Have you ever felt bad or Guilty about your drinking?
E—Have you ever felt you needed a drink first thing in the morning to steady your nerves or get rid of a hangover? (Eye-opener)

When potential alcoholics answer two or more of these questions with a yes, this questionnaire has a sensitivity of 93 percent and a specificity of 76 percent for identification of problem drinkers. In other words, two or more yeses indicate that the person likely has crossed the boundary between temperate use of alcohol and intemperate use of alcohol.

How does that help you if you feel that your spouse may have crossed a boundary with another person or if you wish to analyze whether your own actions are within acceptable limits? The CAGE has been modified by others to broaden its usage. For example, in 1995 Dr. Richard L. Brown and L. A. Rounds published in the *Wisconsin Medical Journal* a version of CAGE that conjointly screens for drug problems as well as alcohol problems. That version is referred to as CAGE-AID.

Though I have not empirically validated my modification of CAGE that I present here, anecdotal evidence from my work with thousands of couples tells me that I am definitely on the right track and that the CAGE-BEAM is worthwhile.

## The CAGE-BEAM

The CAGE-BEAM serves as a screening tool to evaluate whether relationships may have crossed boundaries. It is used as a questionnaire for people who are in a committed relationship with one person but possibly in an inappropriate relationship with another person. The questions specifically ask how the respondent feels about his or her interaction with the "other" person. (Notice that in the CAGE-BEAM, the meaning of "E" is changed from the original CAGE.)

*Is this the person you want to talk with when you are feeling high/excited/happy or when you are feeling low/worried/unhappy?*

C—Have you ever felt you should Cut back on your friendship or relationship with this person (for example, the time you spend with this person, the things you do with this person, or the things you talk to this person about)?

A—Have people Annoyed you by questioning or criticizing your friendship/relationship with this person?

G—Have you ever felt bad or Guilty about your friendship or relationship with this person (for example, the time you spend

talking to this person, or anything you've ever said to, heard
from, or done with this person)?

E—Has this person ever been your Elevator? In other words,
is this the person you want to talk with when you are feeling
high/excited/happy or when you are feeling low/worried/
unhappy?

I remember a church that called me about their concern over the
relationship their minister had developed with his secretary. The minister vehemently denied that anything inappropriate or improper was
occurring, and the church leaders were not sure whether his complain-
ing wife had a valid concern or if she was being unreasonably jealous.
I asked them to use the CAGE-BEAM questionnaire to determine
the likelihood of the minister's involvement with his secretary having
crossed appropriate boundaries.

The leaders replied that they could not know if the minister was
answering those questions honestly or not. I agreed that when an individual was personally concerned about his or her relationship with
another potentially becoming too close, he or she would be much more
likely to answer the questions with transparency. On the other hand, if
the respondent wanted to hide his relationship with another, he likely
would be dishonest in his answers. However, I pointed out to them that
they could likely answer two of the questions by observation. Did he
become annoyed when anyone questioned his relationship with his secretary, and was she the person he wanted to talk to or be with when he
was up or down? They replied that they had observed both to be true.

My counsel?

Based on my experience with people, I suggested that there was a
three-out-of-four chance that he had become too close to his secretary,
violating his marriage covenant by sharing a part of himself with her
that should have been shared only with his wife. They thanked me, decided that I was wrong, and went on as if everything was okay.

Within ninety days the minister left his wife, the secretary left her
husband, and they moved to another town to live with each other.

The CAGE questionnaire possibly could be modified to examine whether a person is becoming so involved in his or her career that it supersedes other responsibilities such as marriage or family, or even to evaluate possible addictions to food, hobbies, or anything else. While there is not ample statistical research proving its efficacy in each of these areas, I feel comfortable using it as a snapshot assessment for all of these situations, at least to the point of looking more carefully at a situation if two or more yes answers occur.

Think about it in terms of Will and Jeanette. It certainly would have been valid with them. If Will had been willing, he could have used the CAGE well before he did to become honest about what was developing with Jeanette. Would that have stopped him? Only if he had the personal strength and integrity to face the truth about himself and what he was doing. Could Rita have used her observation of CAGE to act more quickly to work to save her marriage? Yes, if she had known enough about Jeanette to determine from her own observation whether Will was annoyed when she expressed her concerns about Jeanette and whether he was now using her as his elevator rather than his own wife. If she could have observed that, and trusted her instincts to press the matter, she may have short-circuited the process.

However, she should not feel guilty. All too many spouses either do not trust their instincts about this or fear that they will drive their mates away if they do press the issue. My view is that there is a way to do this effectively (and I will tell you about it in Chapter 10, "Learning to Love Anew").

## "IT AIN'T OVER TILL IT'S OVER"

When is a marriage really over? When does it cease to be worth fighting for?

I have seen men and women respond to damaged marriages in every way imaginable. Many will fight to the bitter end. Others will bail out the instant it becomes clear that a spouse has cheated. Some will retreat into their misery, willing to live the rest of their lives behind walls of silence, even if that means allowing a spouse to have serial affairs or even behave abusively.

I believe these two premises about marriage:

*Any marriage can be lost.* I have met people who believe their social standing, religious beliefs, good character, charmed life, or good family name makes them divorce proof. From many years of working with couples, I can assure you that no marriage is beyond risk. Politician, preacher, plumber, or pianist, it makes no difference. Marriages from every social standing, every lifestyle, every ethnicity, and every religion fail. That is why I encourage even the most happily married couples to consciously move along the LovePath from attraction to acceptance to attachment to aspiration.

*Any marriage can be saved.* I met a husband and wife who told me they were married for twenty-five years without ever experiencing romantic love. After one of our courses, they wrote to ask me, "Where were you twenty-five years ago? We're madly in love now, for the very first time!"

I ran into another couple in a hotel one day. They had attended a class I had developed for churches some weeks earlier, because their marriage was dead and all but buried. They were living in separate bedrooms and getting ready to file for divorce. They signed up for our class, The Path to Soul-Satisfying Love, only because of the intense pressure of their friends, but they stuck it out and it revolutionized their relationship. In the course, they had seen me on video and, therefore, recognized me as I crossed the lobby that later day in a hot. They stopped me to tell me their story and how their marriage had turned around completely. They were checking into the hotel because they were on their second honeymoon.

> *Any marriage has the potential to offer a love so powerful that it becomes a type of heaven on earth. That very same marriage also has the potential to become a darkened dungeon.*

How can any marriage be saved? Well, two things have to happen.

First, each must stop doing the things destroying the marriage. In other words they have to quit backtracking down the LovePath.

Second, each must begin to do again the things that lead in the right direction on the LovePath.

Any marriage has the potential to offer a love so powerful that it becomes a type of heaven on earth. That very same marriage also has the potential to become a darkened dungeon. If a man and a woman loved one another before—or even if they believe that they have never loved each other—they can fall in love and be more in love than ever.

It will not be easy. It will mean both people have to be willing to give and take. New patterns of living together must be learned. However, the result will be the love you have always yearned for. It will be the fulfillment of your heart through a giving partner, and a partner to whom you can also give. There is no joy in life that is any sweeter.

"But we just can't get along," you might interject. Couples tell me how they fuss and fight constantly. Divorce courts have presented us with a familiar term: irreconcilable differences. After we do months, years, even decades of battle, some of the most patient and determined among us are prone to believe that we really do have irreconcilable differences. And yet, are they really irreconcilable? Is there some way to get past them and find a way to live happily together? Yes. I believe I can help you with that business of reconciling differences. I will start in the next chapter.

## WILL, RITA, AND JEANETTE

So how did Will, Rita, and Jeanette turn out? As with the other stories in this book, they are a composite of several stories, so I will tell you how these stories typically play out.

Will might have left with Jeanette, but if he had, the odds of their relationship lasting long-term were very, very poor. Once limerence runs its course, the thrill of courtship turns into the everyday life of marriage. Formerly invisible or ignored flaws finally come into view, often aggravatingly so. Will would one day—likely about three years into his romance with Jeanette—come to his senses and realize all he had walked away from to have his lover.

Being a father a couple weekends a month is very different from living in the same house as your children. It might sound like a satisfying arrangement when one is in the heat of limerence, but when that condition ends, as it must, most moms or dads find it miserable to be the "other parent" or even the single parent raising the kids. After all, your children did not ask to be born. You brought them into this world. It is not they who owe you safety, guidance, and love, but it is you who owe them.

I am still scandalized every time I hear some man or woman so easily dismiss that responsibility by saying something like, "Well, this is really better for the children." No. That is nothing more than rationalization so that you can abandon your responsibilities to those who need you more than they need anything else on this earth. Children need parents who are together and who put their children's welfare ahead of their own. Every child born deserves that; few get it.

*Children need parents who are together and who put their children's welfare ahead of their own. Every child born deserves that; few get it.*

Additionally, sacrificing your religious or moral beliefs and values eventually leads you to do one of two things: you become a different person than you were before or you are broken by living in contradiction to your beliefs. Maybe both.

I have seen so many who left their spouses for their lovers eventually be abandoned by that lover, even if they married. Why? You often hear it like this: "You aren't the same person I fell in love with." That is much truer than you might imagine. When people live in contradiction to their beliefs and values, they become a different person in so many ways. How can they continue to be who they were when they no longer live by the code that once guided their lives?

In short, they cannot.

In our Marriage Helper turnaround weekend workshop, I have seen hundreds of people hit with that realization. "I'm giving up people and beliefs that have been a crucial part of my life for my lover. I cannot do this and continue to be the person my lover fell in love with. I don't even know if I can continue to love myself." That is one of the reasons why three out of four couples that attend our workshop salvage their marriages and work out good relationships, even those who came with the intention of leaving with their lovers as soon as the workshop ended. They only came to get their pastor, kids, parents, or friends off their back, yet they leave with the tools, desire, and motivation to make their marriages work.

Will and Rita would fit into that category. Maybe you would, too. If you are in love with someone else and find that the thought of any workshop that might motivate you to save your marriage is terrifying, then you are the very person who needs to attend. If, during the three days of our workshop, you decide not to leave your spouse for your lover, we will have done you the greatest favor—and saved you from the greatest misery—that you can imagine.

In other words, if our workshop convinces you not to leave, then you need to know that now rather than later. If your lover was smart, he or she should demand that you accompany your spouse to the workshop and find out.

### CHAPTER SUMMARY

- Being in the attachment stage of the LovePath does not assure that you will always stay there. Some people backtrack down the LovePath, losing love for the other person.
- Backtracking occurs when apathy causes attachment to weaken, acceptance to wane, and attraction to waver.
- If a person goes forward on the LovePath with any person, he or she will fall in love with that person even if one or both are married or committed to someone else. Limerence for that person is likely to occur.

- Affairs can take place whenever a spouse is replaced by anything, not just another person.
- To know if you have crossed boundaries, use the CAGE-BEAM questionnaire.
- Any marriage can be lost.
- Any marriage can be saved if
  - each person stops doing things destroying the relationship
  - each person does the things to move forward on the LovePath

# THE CHALLENGE
# OF CONFLICT

*The opening sentence* to Leo Tolstoy's *Anna Karenina* reads, "All happy families resemble one another; each unhappy family is unhappy in its own way." To some extent, that statement is true. At least, it *feels* as if no one in the world could understand our pain. We feel completely alone, helpless, and isolated.

On the other hand, those of us who study marriage know that unhappy families are not as unique as they think they are. Many of the same patterns of frustration occur in homes everywhere.

What we find is that partners do not know how to handle their disagreements and disputes positively. They seem to get caught up in the same futile cycles repeatedly: the sore topic comes up yet again, he makes his usual cutting remarks, and she retaliates with her own. Round and round it goes, and where it stops, everyone knows: nowhere. Nothing is settled. The whole messy confrontation simply leaves everyone frustrated and wounds innocent bystanders (children, for example) as well as those directly involved.

Sometimes couples come to feel that it is not even worth going into battle anymore. There is an unspoken truce, the arguments are put aside, but there is no peace—not really. Marriages are not supposed to be guided by conditions of truce. Husband and wife are not meant to be like two countries that respect each other's borders and avoid one another. They are meant to be one, indivisible, with freedom and justice for all. Real peace is more than an uneasy truce or the absence of battle. It is active unity. It is the ability to work out things so that everyone is happy.

How do you handle anger? How do you handle arguments? Would you like to be freed from the vicious cycle that always hurts and never helps? Read on. The material that follows is a small section of what we present in our Marriage Helper workshop. We know from consistent feedback that it is among the most helpful and practical strategies that we have to offer.

## THE SOURCE OF ANGER

If you are angry about something, most likely there is something lying beneath that emotion: pain. When a relationship has problems, someone has suffered a wound or a series of them. The problem is there is no Band-Aid for what we feel inside. There is no pill that goes to the source of the problem and dissolves the issue. Two of us must work together to do that, and sometimes we fail. The result of that failure is pain that abides.

*Pain that leads to anger generally comes from one of three categories.*

Frank Scott, PhD, director of the Counseling Center at Madison Church of Christ, taught me a great deal about how to understand anger and the underlying pains that cause it. He says the pain that leads to anger generally comes from one of three categories.

- *Loss.* Loss brings about pain and eventually anger. It comes whether we lose a person, a position, a place, or anything else important to us. We may feel pain from the loss of our youth and energy and innocence. We inevitably lose health and some of our looks, and we lose opportunities that gave us hope. There are cases when the unthinkable happens, and a couple loses a child. You might think the two of them would cling together in that event, but in so many cases there is pain, there is anger, and there is an inability to comfort each other. A couple that loses a child may soon lose their marriage, adding tragedy upon tragedy. There are so many kinds of loss, so many varieties of pain that result, and so much anger that springs from that pain.

- *Violation of expectations.* We have dreams and great expectations that we believe will become a reality. If we did not, what sad and hope-challenged people we would be. Nevertheless, life takes twists and turns that we never expect. Some children lose their rightful expectation of being protected and loved because someone violates them. Some people marry with expectations of what their spouses will accomplish in life, and feel pain and anger when their spouses miss the mark dramatically. In one case I know of, the woman's intense excitement and participation in sex before marriage gave her husband-to-be the expectation of that kind of sexual intensity throughout their married life. He became hurt and very angry when that did not happen. When we do not get what we expect, we might blame a partner, we might blame life itself, but either way, we are angry.

- *Violation of trust.* There is no feeling of hurt like the experience of having someone we love betray our trust. We let down our guard, exposed our hearts, and allowed the other to see into the deepest part of us, only to discover that it was not the safe thing to do. We need to know that those we trust will always be trustworthy, no matter what, and we experience great pain and anger when they betray us.

Pain in itself is never welcome, but it is least welcome when it comes from the person we most love. We can handle our bitterness toward the boss at work by getting another job, or simply by going home every night and enjoying the weekend. It is not as easy to run away from someone who lives in the same home and sleeps in the same bed.

Sometimes that kind of pain drives us toward self-medication. What are the choices? Alcohol or drugs, compulsive overeating, extramarital affairs, or some other form of escapism. It may begin simply, with a few extra drinks or a little allegedly innocent flirting. If these patterns of behavior give some relief from pain, some way to escape at least for a little while the stresses and hurts of life, they often lead to addiction. Of course, the addiction, which began as a refuge from pain, brings more pain. It will eventually destroy the marriage itself, and the addict as well.

That problem is a serious one—even a life-threatening one—and the subject for another book entirely. If you recognize yourself or the one you love in this description, you should immediately seek professional counseling and/or medical care for addiction. For now let us make the point that pain may come from elsewhere, but we ourselves are always responsible for how we respond. That is the root of the word *responsible*.

Avoiding or overcoming addiction means facing our pain squarely and finding healing with the help of the right people.

# THE PRODUCTION AND PATH OF ANGER

Think again about a time you were enraged. Where did you focus your anger? In all probability, you focused it on somebody, likely the individual who had done something to you. We tend to project our anger, and all our angry thoughts, toward others. It is true that people treat us terribly at times. They betray us, they use us, and they say hurtful things.

What we often fail to realize, however, is that the person who causes us the most pain is that person who appears in the mirror. Think about it. Life happens to us, event by event. We choose how to frame those events in our minds.

Imagine that you are driving along in traffic on the way to a meeting. Suddenly, a little red sports car pops right in front of you and you have to hit the brakes to keep from hitting it. The red car slows down a couple of times, looking for a turn, but remains in front of you. Then it slows down as you approach a traffic light, and takes just enough time passing under it to make you miss the light.

How would you react? You may be irritated at the beginning, and then become more and more angry. If incensed enough, you may even run the red light to catch up with this automotive persecutor and shake your fist at him!

*His actions may have triggered anger within you, but it is* your *anger, not his, and you have a choice of whether or not to let your anger take over.*

The irritation you feel is normal, but whatever anger you feel is yours, not that of the driver of the other car. You may shout, "That guy made me mad!" In reality, no one can *make* you do anything. Emotions rise from within. His actions may have triggered anger within you, but it is *your* anger, not his, and you have a choice of whether or not to let your anger take over. Rather than becoming angry enough to do something dumb, it is possible for you to tell yourself, "That driver is a jerk! But he's not going to ruin my day. I will not give him that power. Nor will I break a law and endanger my life on account of uncontrolled emotions."

*Framing* is the way you view or understand something, and it is amazing how different framing produces different results. In an interesting psychological experiment done in Germany, researchers offered two sets of subjects the approximate equivalent of one hundred dollars. They asked each group to gamble the money, but the framing was different for each group. To the first group the directions were, "If you choose not to gamble the money, you automatically lose 60 percent of the money."

Nearly all of them gambled. To the second group the directions were, "If you choose not to gamble the money, you may keep 40 percent anyway." Hardly any of them gambled. The fascinating fact here is that each group was offered the exact same deal, but the first group focused on what they would lose, while the second group focused on what they would gain. Same truth, same fact, but different framing.

Now apply that to what makes you angry. The driver of the red sports car was obviously wrong, but it is all in how you choose to frame it that will determine how you will react to it. If you see it as personal—"He did that to me!"—then you are likely to get angry. If you view it as impersonal—"He's an idiot who's going to have an accident or get a ticket"—you can go on about your business and not even think about him again.

Rather than thinking about how hurt you are by the actions of others, frame it in a way that gives you the ability to either control your anger or not get angry at all. Sometimes that means seeing it from the other person's perspective. "I can see why she said that; it wasn't to hurt me but because she is frustrated and isn't handling it well." Sometimes it is dismissing it as a personal attack on you and seeing it as a problem the other person has. Whatever the framing, you can decide to see things in such a way that either prevents or reduces your anger because it takes your focus from your personal pain to a broader objectivity.

Sometimes we have that moment of decision—will we give in to anger or not? Do not see anger as something over which you have no control. You will be amazed about how good it feels to let that burden slip off your shoulders. The truth about anger and bitterness is that we are the victims. It is also true that the reason we need to forgive people is not because they deserve it (they actually may not); it is because it is healthier for us not to have that emotional cancer eating away at our insides.

Somewhere inside you lies an "anger bank." It is like a big room in your memory that is filled with files—grievances and hurts. Some of us keep very detailed files, and that anger bank requires more and more of our emotional energy to maintain. But why? What good are all those records of wrongs? Keeping that bank active keeps you on the edge of anger, because it keeps you in touch with your pain in an unhealthy way. Remember that you are the leading manufacturer of your own pain, and the sole distributor of your anger. You are the one who decides whether to let something or someone get you down.

Doubt that?

Consider how your parents managed their anger. Most of the time we find that we handle it like one of them. Think about your mother and father or whoever it was who raised you. What were the anger management styles of each of them? Which one are you the most like? Was the way that he or she handled anger helpful or hurtful? Do you really want to handle your anger similarly, or would you rather be mature enough to handle it in a better, more effective way?

These are not rhetorical questions. Decide if your anger response is patterned after that of one of your parents and if that is a good or bad thing for you and those around you.

My friend Dr. Frank Scott says there are three ways that people handle anger:

- *Anger-Outs.* These are the shouters and the door-slammers. If you are not an Anger-Out, you feel very uncomfortable around those who are. They do not keep their anger to themselves; they have no natural filter for it. Anger-Outs show their emotions outwardly, whether in sarcasm or something more overt. At least you know exactly where they stand. The misconception about Anger-Outs is that they are much healthier—they get that anger right out of their system, and they are better off for it. That is not true. Doing that actually stirs up anger in us. We believe we are getting something off our chest, but we are as likely to be angry tomorrow or the next day. We must also consider the damage that is done (much of it verbal) when we blow our tops. We damage things and feelings. And people.
- *Anger-Ins.* You can guess who makes up the next group. Anger-Ins are people who hate to show their feelings on the outside. It is said that still waters run deep, and calm; placid

160 STEP THREE: ATTACHMENT

people tend to have deeper emotions than we think. Anger-Ins sulk, withdraw, and hold grudges. However, just because their anger is suppressed does not mean that it is not any less dangerous. Nor will it simply disperse after its statute of limitations runs out. The danger for Anger-Ins is that the anger ultimately expresses itself irrationally. It comes out in some indirect, unexpected form that we call passive-aggressive anger. Have you ever had that nagging feeling that someone is smiling at you, acting perfectly neighborly, yet quietly making your life miserable? You might be encountering passive-aggressive anger.

• *Anger-Controls.* We all tend to be one of the above, because none of us is perfect. Nobody acts out all anger, and no one holds it in every single time. We use both styles, though we will tend toward one. Hopefully, we will also try the third alternative, the wise management of our anger. Unfortunately, only a few people are primarily Anger-Controls. These individuals have anger, just like everyone else. However, they handle it appropriately and maturely. Fewer tasks are more difficult, but the right approach is to express anger directly (the opposite of passive-aggressive anger, which deflects the emotion in a false direction). You do not explode; you do not withdraw to sulk; you do not kick the dog or attack a substitute; you do not suppress or bury your feelings. Instead, you express your anger verbally and as respectfully as possible. Key phrase: "I feel angry with you because . . ." It helps to try to find the right time when everyone is calm, and to stick to the issue at hand. Then simply explain your point of view. You will find that many sources of anger can be managed and solved, and you will be mentally healthier and happier for it.

> *The danger for Anger-Ins is that the anger ultimately expresses itself irrationally.*

## The Fight That Solves Nothing

I have noticed that when most couples argue and fight, they wind up in a familiar pattern, no matter what began the argument. I picture it as a circle. It makes little difference where a couple enters the circle; once they start they go through the whole gamut of their normal, ineffective, painful-without-solution argument circle—round and round. Interestingly, the entire process could be short-circuited and changed to a discussion that actually would bring about a solution if only one of them decided not to enter the circle.

That's right. It is as simple as not participating in the argument in the same old way but approaching it differently. That one approach would change a relationship for the better.

When explaining this to couples in conflict, I illustrate with the four ways of fighting/arguing identified by Dr. John Gottman at the University of Washington's Love Lab. He calls them the *Four Horsemen.*

He is not speaking of the famous ones in the Bible, those Four Horsemen of the Apocalypse who bring terrible things to the world. These are the four ways we inflict the most damage upon each other in everyday conversation. Dr. Gottman has identified four leading indicators that a marriage will fail.

As I share these four insights with couples, they recognize each of the Horsemen and realize how it has harmed their relationship. Quite frequently, they point to the recognition and control of these horsemen as very liberating. Moreover, it is all so simple. Can you navigate your way through an evening of conversation without saddling up one of these four? How about a week? If you can do that, the changes in your relationship will be radical indeed.

Let us get to know the four.

## The Four Horsemen of Anger

*1. Criticism. One of the surest predictors of a failed marriage is criticism—the consistent putting-down of one partner. For example,*

*"You always say you're going to do something, but you never get around to it." "You never know what you're talking about."*

Dr. Gottman believes that most marital conflicts begin with criticism. When something is on your mind, should you ignore it? Sometimes that could be a wise and loving idea. I think it is always worthwhile to stop and think, "Do I really want an argument over this? Is this really worth fighting about?" If the answer is no, let it go. You do not have to win every battle to win the war.

*One of the surest predictors of a failed marriage is criticism— the consistent putting-down of one partner.*

If you decide something is worth dealing with, even if it has the potential of causing conflict, deal with it through the process of a complaint rather than through criticism. The difference is that a complaint focuses on *specific behavior* and avoids general character assassination or blame. It is fair to discuss one instance at a time, and to do it in a non-accusatory way. We go wrong when we try to create some overarching pattern of bad character or habits in our mate. That, of course, is unfair and inappropriate. She may feel a degree of anger because he has sloppy habits, and she may tend to express that anger through criticizing: "You are such a slob! You never pick up behind yourself!" She may have a point, but she is unlikely to get the best results when approaching the subject this way.

A better idea would be to point out the specific instance of sloppy behavior, and ask her husband to help her out in the future by being neater. "Honey, you left your underwear on the floor again. Be a sweetie and pick them up and put them in the hamper." If she could do that rather than indicating that he has a problem, she would be dealing with specific behavior and not making it sound as if something is wrong with him. It is a much better approach to avoid fighting and actually to get your spouse to hear what is important to you and to act accordingly.

What are your most common criticisms of your spouse? How could you better handle these situations?

*2. Contempt. According to Dr. Gottman, this is the most evil and dangerous of the Four Horsemen. It is a more serious infraction than criticism because it involves disrespect. Remember, respect is the most essential element at the center of a relationship.*

We show contempt when we insult someone. In our marriage vows, we likely promised to "love and honor," and contempt is precisely the opposite of honor—it conveys disgust. At least criticism can be made constructive if we change it to a complaint by focusing it on specific behavior. Contempt, however, is all about the *person* and what is wrong with him or her. It displays itself in various ways, such as sarcasm, a sneering or mocking tone, the rolling of eyes, hostile humor, and anything else that gives the impression that "this is so typical of you because you're not much good."

Contempt is letting our anger shape our approach in a hurtful way, as if we have the right to scoff at or scorn the other because she or he is so flawed. It never leads to anything good and nearly always leads to something bad.

*3. Defensiveness. When we feel we are being attacked, we are likely to use various defense mechanisms. Defensiveness is a tool for deflection: "I'm not the problem—YOU are!" In other words it's a counterattack, a reflex response to criticism or contempt.*

"Why do you always come home drunk?" she demands. "What's wrong with you?"

He becomes defensive. "It's because you don't understand me. You treat me poorly all the time, so I have to go somewhere and get loaded."

Defensiveness is often a Horseman sent out to do battle with another Horseman—you criticize, I defend.

*Defensiveness is often a Horseman sent out to do battle with another Horseman—you criticize, I defend. What happens, of course, is that the battle escalates.*

What happens, of course, is that the battle escalates. Once he accuses her of treating him poorly, she is going to retaliate with a further attack upon his character.

Defensiveness sometimes shows itself as excuse making and denial of responsibility, and these approaches do not satisfy the partner doing the criticizing. Round and round it goes. Defensiveness, though a natural human reaction, never leads to resolution, only to more intense argument.

*4. Stonewalling. Some people engage in battle indirectly by resorting to stonewalling. They simply refuse to respond. Perhaps it's a person's natural tendency, being an Anger-In. Maybe it's that the stonewaller doesn't have a good excuse or defense. Or it may be passivity calculated to irritate the partner. After all, no one likes being ignored. It makes others angry when we look away from them, or down, or if we quietly leave the room. Tuning someone out is just another form of contempt, isn't it?*

Most of the time, we do not resort to silence for well-intentioned reasons. No, we walk away when we do not want to talk about something unpleasant or we do not want to face something we know should be changed.

A biblical proverb says, "A soft answer turns away wrath" (Proverbs 15:1). In other words, the best policy is to put out the fire slowly by cooperating with gentleness, respect, and no defensiveness. When we simply refuse to talk about things, we are opting out of the very arrangement of marriage, of having unity.

Interestingly, in our work with couples through the years, we have seen that men have a high tendency to be stonewallers.

## WATCHING FOR THE HORSEMEN

Did you recognize yourself among those four responses to anger? I hope you resisted the temptation to look for the other person's negative tendencies, and instead focused on your own. Real change begins within us.

I teach couples to go over the Four Horsemen and evaluate how often they turn up in disputes. Then I ask them to go home in the evening and agree on a pact to have a "Horseman-free" evening. Whenever one partner hears the beginning of criticism, contempt, defensiveness, or stonewalling, he or she gently says, "Horseman." The other person is not allowed to respond that what he is doing is not a Horseman, because the very denial can become a Horseman in itself. If the other person hears what you are saying, or interprets what you are doing, as a Horseman, then it *is*, for that person, a Horseman.

Avoid the Horsemen. Change your approach to anger by using a more positive strategy for dealing with the issue of the moment. You have nothing to lose and everything to gain.

Many couples adopt the "Horseman Watch" to their permanent conversational patterns. As a result, they see the barriers to love fade away over time, and eventually they don't need to worry about those four angry mounted soldiers any longer.

## THE KEY ROLE OF FORGIVENESS

So how does a couple talk with each other without anger or unfruitful arguing? How can they get to solutions for their disagreements or problems?

Though it may sound trite, the most important thing is to try, as best we can, to understand the other person—what she feels, what she really is trying to communicate, and the source of her pain. We have mentioned respect repeatedly in this book. It is essential to any relationship's growth, satisfaction, fulfillment, and longevity.

> *How does a couple get to solutions for their disagreements or problems?*

There is one more thing to add that we should talk about now: forgiveness.

When couples attend our Marriage Helper, they usually come with great pain and, therefore, great anger. We hear comments such as, "As much as what he did hurt, what hurts more is that he lied to me!" or "She deceived our friends, our family, our children," or "I can't believe that he would choose her over me. I don't know that I could ever make love to him again because I would wonder if he were thinking about her."

The list, of course, goes on and on. Imagine any hurt that you can think of and we have likely heard it. Sometimes it involves hurt from being deceived, sometimes from being rejected, or sometimes from how one spouse treated the children (or a specific child), especially if they are a stepfamily.

How does anyone get past deep hurts? Does time really heal all wounds? Is there something else that must happen in addition to the passing of time? Absolutely.

Forgiveness.

Often, when we reach this point in a workshop, someone points out that they are not ready to forgive, or that they have tried to forgive and cannot. Usually those statements mean that the person who is hurt has not lost that hurt or the anger coming from that hurt. They think that forgiveness is an emotion and because that emotion is not occurring, they believe that they are not forgiving at all.

But here's the truth: forgiveness is *not* an emotion. It is a decision. Forgiveness is a decision that will, with time, affect emotions; it is not an emotion that will affect decisions.

Notice that there are three words that keep coming up as we discuss each part of the LovePath: *truth*, *respect*, and *decisions*. As we discussed acceptance, I shared with you the importance of allowing your lover to tell you the truth, even if you do not like what you hear. It is just as important that you tell the truth always. Truth indeed sets you free.

Throughout the book, we have returned repeatedly to the concept of treating the other person with respect, always accepting thoughts and feelings as valid even if they contradict your own, and never attempting to control the other person. That does not, of course, mean that you have to accept all the behaviors of the other person. You make it safe for them to be themselves in the way they think or feel, but you do not have to allow behavior that is destructive to you, to them, to the relationship, or to anyone else. There are boundaries in life that must be respected.

Everything we discussed really comes to a matter of making a decision. While you cannot control your emotions with a firm and unshakable hand, you can make decisions and follow through on them, no matter what you feel. You can decide to give respect, to tell the truth, to allow your mate to tell the truth, and to accept what the other thinks or feels. You can do that even when hurt, angry, or feeling any other emotion. Actually, it is that very ability that leads to maturity, making the right decision even when you do not want to.

As for forgiveness, it's a set of three decisions.

First, decide to view the other person as a flawed human being rather than evil personified. When you put another into that category, you do not continue to vilify them because you realize that you, too, are flawed. This does not mean that you necessarily view your own behavior to be as harmful as the other person's—though maybe in some cases you should—but that you simply no longer think them to be the devil or the devil's kin. By granting them the right to be a human, however flawed, you can find the ability to make the second decision.

Second, decide that you will not take vengeance, even if that is your right. Sometimes I say it this way: give up your right to hurt the other person in return for the hurt done to you. It is okay to demand justice—if someone steals my car, I will prosecute—but do not try to gain vengeance. I define vengeance as trying to make the other person hurt as badly as you hurt. That never works. You can never be sure that the other person hurts as badly

*Give up your right to hurt the other person in return for the hurt done to you.*

as you do. Moreover, even if you did make them hurt that way, the very act of causing that hurt likely does something to your own sense of being a decent and caring human being.

You see, forgiveness is never for the benefit of the other person. It is always for you. It sets you free from the ball and chain holding you to the person on whom you want to exact vengeance. By seeing the other as flawed and giving up your right to hurt that person, you can be free of him or her. You go on with your life, no longer tied to the other or what he or she did.

Third—and this step is optional—restore or develop a relationship with the person who hurt you. This is where forgiving becomes more divine than human. If someone were to steal my car, I would forgive him or her by the first two steps so that I would not be angry and turn bitter. By forgiving, I set myself free. However, I can't say I'd go down to the prison and develop a relationship with the thief so that when he'd served his time, we could become fishing buddies. There is no need, and certainly no desire on my part, for that. However, what if it were my daughter who hurt me in some way? What about my parent? Best friend? Spouse? In those relationships, there may well be a better future for each of us if I do make the third step and decide to restore the relationship.

The day that I wrote the paragraphs above, I was on one of the most popular radio stations in Nashville, Tennessee, with their morning drive-time personalities, Woody and Jim. Every month they invite me on for an hour or so to take calls about relationships. On this particular morning a lady called to ask if she should consider forgiving her husband for his affair and taking him back as he was asking her to do. I helped her think through all there was to gain if she tried, to understand the risk if she does, and to consider what she stands to lose if she doesn't.

It is always a risk to redevelop a relationship with someone who hurt you badly. And yet, it did not take her long to see that the advantages of forgiving and moving to a new level far exceeded the risk involved.

Forgiveness clears the air, sets the table afresh, and gives you a chance to move forward rather than being tied to the past.

It is essential to overcoming anger and adversity and getting back on the LovePath.

## FROM ANGER TO JOY

Perhaps you have been in a struggling relationship. Perhaps you are in one even now. Think hard about the concepts we have explored in this chapter. I would encourage you to read it more than once and to write down your idea of how each concept relates to your life and your patterns of relationship.

Think about the journey we have made from anger to genuine love.

What if we could clearly understand, for the very first time, what makes us angry, and how to manage those emotions? What if we could make dead certain that Gottman's Four Horsemen—criticism, contempt, defensiveness, and stonewalling—never rode through our conversations again? What if we found those tension points that make it so hard for us to talk honestly, and spent time working them out together?

What if we could forgive—not expecting all the emotions to change immediately but making a decision to go through forgiveness's steps—and gradually overcome our hurt, replacing it with love and happiness?

What if we found that we could really communicate once again, just as we did at the very beginning? What if we actually began eagerly to anticipate talking to each other every evening?

Well, if we could do all that—and, by learning the art of being in love, we absolutely can!—then our relationships would be like fresh, fragrant gardens in the morning, when the sun first rises and the blooms begin turning toward the sun. The colors of the flowers would be lovelier than ever.

Love is so much like a garden. It takes a bit of tending. We must get our hands a little dirty, and we must learn to stoop low. But oh! The beauty of the result is like nothing else on earth.

**CHAPTER SUMMARY**

Though conflict may occur anywhere along the LovePath, it is particularly important to know how to properly handle conflict if you want to maintain attachment. There are several steps to help you with this.

*Understand Anger*
- Anger always comes from pain. Look past the anger to the underlying pain.
- We tend to handle anger in a way similar to one of our parents.
- Where anger comes from:
  - Loss
  - Violation of expectation
  - Violation of trust

*Understand the Three Ways to Handle Anger*
- Anger-Outs—show anger toward others but not in a way helpful to the self or the situation.
- Anger-Ins—keep anger inside until it expresses itself inappropriately.
- Anger-Controls—manage anger wisely to handle it appropriately and maturely.

*Understand the Trap of Arguing Unproductively*
- Stay out of the conflict circle.
- Avoid the Four Horsemen.
  - Criticism—communicates "what is wrong with you?"
  - Contempt—communicates disrespect
  - Defensiveness—communicates "What do you mean, what's wrong with me? What's wrong with *you?*"

- Stonewalling—refusing to respond to the other and, therefore, escalating the conflict

*Understand the Power of Forgiveness*
- Decide to see the other as a flawed human rather than evil.
- Decide to give up your right to hurt the one who hurt you. Let go of vengeance.
- Reconcile (optional).

# STEP FOUR:
# ASPIRATION

*9*

# THE FULFILLMENT
# OF INTIMACY

*I wish you* could know Alice, my wife. She's incredibly special to me. Therefore, whenever I meet someone new, my first thought is that this person needs to know Alice. You see, when I look at my wife, I see many things. I see a lifetime of love, dressed in Alice's clothing. I see my companion—the walking, smiling embodiment of my entire adult journey and all the tears and laughter and discovery we have shared.

That's a lot to see in one person, isn't it? Sure, I realize you would never see all those things in her, because you don't happen to be me. You haven't been there. You haven't shared the nearly four-decade adventure that Alice and I have lived out. But we have. We've seen it through, sometimes with a great deal of pain, sometimes with inexpressible joy. For that reason, we have become highly significant to each other. I'm being sincere when I tell you that it's not even remotely possible for us to take each other for granted at this stage. Why? Because of the long path that we've traveled together, all its twists and turns, its high points and low points. That shared journey has woven a bond between two living creatures that is simply unbreakable, and neither of us can now imagine being without the other.

We've walked the path described in this book—virtually every part of it. In each story I've shared is a little of our own story. I imagine you've seen a little of your own as well. Alice and I have known what it is like to be madly in love, and what it's like to be just mad. We've moved along the stepping-stones of the LovePath—in both directions.

We now walk the upward way of increasingly deeper love and intimacy. But there was also a time when we were divorced. There was a time when I didn't believe I loved my wife anymore—and I knew for certain that I didn't love myself. I created unthinkable pain and chaos for both of us. I was on a spiraling path, but it certainly wasn't spiraling upward. I was one miserable human being.

Yet like the downtrodden son in that story told by Jesus, the day arrived when I came to the end of myself and my thoughts turned toward home. I rediscovered the faith in God that I had lost, and that helped me rediscover some semblance of faith in myself.

In the end Alice took me back. The process of forgiveness was not instantaneous. The conditions of reinstatement were not slight. She did exactly what was right: she placed me on probation, making it clear that she would offer me love, a marriage, and a home only if I continued to show myself to be worthy of them. And so we set about rebuilding a marriage that had been destroyed.

*There wasn't a great deal of affection between Alice and me as we started back on the LovePath.*

There wasn't a great deal of affection between Alice and me as we started back on the LovePath. I wanted to be taken back, but I wasn't certain that I still loved, or that I could ever be worthy of being loved. Yet here we are today, more in love than ever. Somehow, even with all the hurt that came between us, we are more passionate about each other than ever. We came through a terrible time, but one day we turned a corner, stepped into a patch of faint sunlight, and found that we were entering a familiar place: the place called attraction.

What a miracle to be there again when there have been so many bitter feelings. You can't really appreciate what it is to be happy until you've truly been unhappy. You don't understand the miracle of forgiveness until you need it desperately—and it's granted to you. You discover that nothing in this world is more precious than the sincere love of one who cares for you when others tell her that she shouldn't.

I've talked with you about the phenomenon of limerence—that mad, passionate obsession to be united with someone. Did Alice and I rediscover that? No, we didn't. But that isn't what we need.

What we need right now is something more mature, something fuller and more profound between us. We want to enjoy each other at our own speed, so to speak. We want to love each other in the midst of the lives we need to lead, being useful to our family, our friends, and the world itself.

It seems we've found one more truth about the LovePath. It's not simply about a relationship with one other person. It's also about a fuller understanding and appreciation of life itself. That means there is a stepping-stone on the LovePath that includes, but goes beyond, the relationship. I call it *aspiration*.

## DREAMING TOGETHER

When I first met my wonderful wife, I got to know her family. I often joke about her father being a "used-mule dealer." He lived in a farm community where plowing the field was a daily way of life. He would go to some farm and find out if they had a mule, a cow, a tractor, or anything else they'd like to sell. He'd get the best deal he could, then take what he'd bought to another farm and try to sell it for a profit. All of this occurred fairly close to home. Her dad was always home for supper. Alice grew up in a secure, structured environment in a small town where she knew everyone.

My life was a little different.

As a young person I wasn't always happy being myself. I was one of those kids who people enjoyed kidding for being so ugly. They still do to this day. As a teen I found that my way to be accepted was to be funny. However, that wasn't enough. I wanted to be cool rather than simply humorous; I wanted admiration rather than amusement. I used to dream that I could do something so people would say good things about me rather than ridiculing me.

That happened with my first speech class in college. I discovered that the natural wit I had developed as a teen seeking acceptance translated into a speaking style that people enjoyed. I could use my wit to get the audience with me, and then speak passionately about truths that had the power to change people's lives. It was a noble calling. What's more, it would give me a way to be accepted and even admired. That dream and motivation was very powerful within me, though I didn't recognize it as such at the time.

After Alice and I married, we found ourselves at cross-purposes. She couldn't understand why I was always looking for opportunities to travel and speak. She saw me as not being supportive enough of the home and the marriage. I saw her as insecure and needing too much attention. Because neither of us understood what was really happening, it took several years to figure out what our conflict was actually about. I had one dream for my adult life; Alice had a very different, even contradictory, dream for her adult life. Each of us was keeping the other from fulfilling those dreams.

*Because neither of us understood how important these desires were to each other, we argued over all types of things.*

We finally figured out where the conflict originated. I realized that my dream was fulfilled in the way that most sensibly translated to my personal gifts, to go on the road, speaking to increasing audiences. Meanwhile, Alice's dream was based on the way she grew up, being the daughter of a small-town trader who might wander over to the next county tomorrow but be back by suppertime. Her dream: stability, safety, a family that was together in the same home every night.

Because neither of us understood how important these desires were to each other, we argued over all types of things, including my travel schedule. I was only hearing her complaints, and not the true needs that were beneath them.

So when did all that change? When we finally saw the power of the life desires each of us had. I learned that what she really was saying was, "I want a family. I want security and stability." She learned that being on a platform speaking or on a TV talking to millions of people wasn't just enjoyable for me—it was my dream.

But there's still a problem here. Can you see what it is?

It's one thing to *understand* the dreams of each other, but it's another to know how we can *fulfill* them when our dreams conflict. She wants me at home; I want me all over the place. Something's got to give.

Let's think a bit more about that. However, to get to the positive we must consider some possible negatives.

## ATTRITION OR ASPIRATION?

As I've learned about each stage of the LovePath, the beauty of this journey has moved me.

I'm an American, and I best understand our own national culture. However, what we're talking about is a global experience, something that happens all over the world, no matter how different the customs and values may be. This is the way we were designed to love. The LovePath is how we come together and find meaning and fellowship as humans; it's where we learn the art of being in love. We become one in spirit, then physically we become one through sexual union. That often brings into existence the children who are our fruit. These children carry our genetic heritage into the future, and they pass on the love that we give them as a legacy.

This powerful living attraction between people is about so much more than simply perpetuating the species. It's about perpetuating our happiness here and now. It's about keeping us growing and expanding, to the very end of this life. In my spiritual views, it is to move to the next life of heaven itself.

Therefore, we arrive at perhaps the most amazing truth about the

LovePath. It has a beginning, but when properly traveled, it comes to no final resting place. Instead, it circles back to its beginning and the cycle begins anew. But this time the cycle is different and deeper, to the degree that we have grown and changed—that is, to the degree that we ourselves are different and deeper. As we grow in fulfillment and in caring, we find ever-new reasons to be attracted to each other. As we continue to open up to each other and become more honest, we find ever-new reasons to accept each other more deeply. That leads to stronger attachment.

If we move from attachment to aspiration, then that leads to a higher level of attraction, and the whole process repeats itself with greater fulfillment and bondedness. Yes, love will go round in circles.

"Ah," you say, "sounds nice, but aren't we telling fairy tales again?" If you think the upward spiral of the LovePath sounds a bit idealistic and unrealistic, like the end of a cheesy romantic novel, it is because we see this phenomenon only rarely. It does happen, but the three alternatives—stagnation, backtracking, or attrition—are far more common.

With the first alternative, *stagnation*, a couple becomes comfortable living in the same home but have no real life together, at least not in terms of sharing intimacy. They may have sex occasionally and might even eat out once in a blue moon. However, neither is deeply bonded to the other and, as far as they know themselves, neither is interested in finding a relationship with someone else. The partner is convenient. Life is settled. They may stay together until death but there has been and will be no deepening of their love, no growth together.

Then there is *backtracking*, the second alternative. As we saw in an earlier chapter, every couple does this to some extent, at some point. Hopefully, it doesn't become the pattern, because the final destination is loveless detachment or an actual severance of the relationship. In either case, there is great pain.

The third alternative is the substitution of control for love. I call this alternative *attrition*, because it slowly but surely eats away at love, eroding it until love finally disappears altogether.

When does attrition happen? When people are too insecure to grant the freedom that love requires. Real love, of course, is a giving and even sacrificial thing. It understands the twin paradoxes that the more we give, the more we receive; the more we seize, the more we lose. But desperate love will sometimes try to take a relationship by force, to build confining walls and hold it in.

I once knew a couple that provided a sad example. The husband simply would not trust his wife. Every day he would leave his workplace at certain times to see if she was where she was supposed to be. She knew that if she looked out the window, there his car would be. He couldn't stand to think that she had the freedom of choice to chart her own movements. He was going to exercise all the control he could.

Can any relationship prosper under those circumstances? Of course not. Love and shackles don't go well together. When we cling too tightly for fear of losing something, we ensure our losing it sooner or later. You discovered this principle the first time you desperately loved someone without your love being returned. Perhaps you turned up the pressure and forced the issue. How did that work out for you?

One of the more confusing things about control is that sometimes it isn't immediately recognizable, even to the person who is doing it. I think of it this way: control can be overt or covert. Overt control is relatively easy to identify:

- One person tells the other what to think or condemns the other for voicing an opinion or thought contradictory to the desire of the controller.
- One person tells the other what to feel, or that what they feel isn't real or valid.
- It can be exerted through yelling, physical coercion, or demeaning insults, slurs, and put-downs.
- Sometimes it involves using sex, money, or other tools to get one's way and ensure the yielding of the controlled person.

As bad as overt control is, it seems that covert control is even more insidious. When one person covertly controls the other, there is plausible deniability that control is happening. An outside observer most likely would see no outward signs of control at all. Why? It is done behind closed doors, often subtly, but is as powerful in ensuring the compliance of the one controlled as the more overt methods.

The worst case I remember is a mother who would not speak to her child if the child did anything that displeased her. The silent treatment could go on for days until the child, feeling abandoned and unlovable, would break down in desperate contrition and beg the mother's forgiveness. That methodology gave the mother amazing control over the way her children acted and even what emotions they would let others see. She saw herself as a gentle mom who never resorted to the brutality of spanking, who offered her children freedom to do as they wished. Her children saw her as distant and inaccessible. They did everything they could to make her love them—but it was never enough. You can imagine the problems they took into marriage and throughout life.

*As bad as overt control is, it seems that covert control is even more insidious.*

I've seen this kind of control with couples as well. One finds a way to let the other know how unhappy he is and uses some form of subtle punishment or unpleasantness anytime his will or wishes aren't obeyed. Those in the relationship learn the signs and learn to obey. They yield to the control to feel peace, to feel loved, to feel that they have worth and value—sometimes, even to be safe.

Whether overt or covert, control reduces the controlled to the position of an inferior. The controller indicates through controlling behaviors that her way is best, her mind is wisest, and her views are absolute. The controlled loses self-respect, self-esteem, and sometimes even the ability to act with free will. I remember a young man whose mother vehemently disagreed with his choice of a wife. Though he went through with the wedding to the young woman, he couldn't bear his mother's displeasure. He abandoned his bride on their honeymoon and filed for annulment. They never spent even one night together.

Mom got her way.

Real love, of course, is not possessive or demanding. It gives freedom, then delights in the growth of the other person. It is the way of hope, the upward spiral toward the best of both of us. Because it represents everything we would aspire to—for ourselves and our loved ones—in this life, we call it aspiration.

I understand control all too well. You remember that my dreams and Alice's were at odds? I tried to fulfill my dreams without honoring hers, and I constantly tried to control her by doing everything I could to make life what I wanted it to be. I wouldn't have thought of myself as controlling, but by arguments, persuading, and sometimes just ignoring what Alice felt, I pretty well got my way. She had to learn to live life as I wanted it rather than our learning to live our lives together, fulfilling what we both wanted. That put me in the position of control and her in the position of yielding.

The fascinating thing is that this control didn't affect only the love Alice had for me as time passed; it also negatively affected the love I felt for her. Though she wasn't very effective at trying to control me in order to fulfil her own life expectations, the fact that she tried—that she wasn't in harmony with what I felt I was called to be and do—made us grow apart. We both suffered. Love faded—and died. Rather than reaching our individual aspirations together as a team, we drifted apart, each seeking fulfillment in his or her own way. We often gave in to each other, resenting it when that had to happen.

We were deep in attrition.

## RECONCILING OUR LIFE DESIRES

If the key word of attrition is *control*, the key word for aspiration is *cooperation*.

Everyone seems to be chasing some kind of carrot on a stick—something that pulls them forward in life. Our dreams get us out of bed and into the new day. It is the crushing of our dreams that kills our spirit and sabotages our relationships.

Even more to the point, problems occur in marriage when our visions for life pull us in conflicting directions.

When I ask people what their dream or life expectation is, the most common response is a quizzical stare. "What do you mean? You talking about the fantasies I had as a kid? That kind of thing?"

No. Dr. John Gottman defines the kind of dream we are discussing as "hopes, aspirations, and wishes that

*If the key word of attrition is* control, *the key word for aspiration is* cooperation.

are part of your identity and give purpose and meaning to your life." Most often, I call them *life desires.*

What did you expect life to be like— in terms of marriage, family, career, success, religion, or any other thing that is important to you—when you became an adult? Not just your wishes, but those things that you felt *had* to happen for you to be fulfilled, for life to be worth living. For me, it wasn't really being on a platform. That was a symbol of what I wanted. I wanted to be important, liked, attractive, and loved. So being on a platform, where I wasn't the ugly kid no one else noticed, was my way to be accepted, maybe even needed, and certainly recognized.

Alice's life dream symbolized affection, safety, warmth, and protection. Those things were a vital part of her identity and purpose. She'd never be happy working outside the home, but wanted to be the homemaker and mother—as was her own mother.

As Gottman points out, our dreams often root in our childhood and represent either warm feelings we want to reproduce or negative feelings we want to avoid. Alice's was the former; mine was the latter. The first problem may come when our partner doesn't recognize what our dreams are, or doesn't understand how important they are to us.

A husband may not understand why his wife is so fanatical about the church choir and why she needs to practice that solo for hours. He hasn't been listening when she talks about what she's dreamed of since childhood: to sing on a stage in front of audiences. As a teenager, she used a hairbrush as her microphone and sang to the mirror. Now she is energized by the opportunity to use her vocal skills in front of a church. Her husband doesn't attend the service and is puzzled when she is upset that he didn't come. He simply doesn't get it. This is her dream, the thing that is part of her identity, who she is. He sees church choir through his own eyes (as something a little boring) rather than through hers (the fulfillment of her dream).

Sometimes there is understanding between couples, but not respect. A wife may think her husband is crazy for putting so much energy into coaching that Pop Warner football team. These are ten-year-old boys playing a game, for goodness sake! Why does her husband stay up late at night scribbling *X*s and *O*s in a notebook? Why is he spending good money on blocking dummies and spray paint for the team helmets? Clearly (to her) her husband needs to grow up. She doesn't understand the enduring desire driving him. For that matter, he may not fully understand it himself but it is a crucial driving force in his life.

So how do we get past this impasse? How do we learn to leave control behind and embrace cooperation? The first step? Sit down to discuss your dreams together. It's wonderful to spend a little time trying to understand each other's motivations and dreams, and how you can support each other. Once we bring our personal goals to the table, they can be incorporated into our marital goals.

In other words the husband will not only attend his wife's church performance but also bring her roses afterward, and even encourage her to try out for the neighborhood theater musical. She, on the other hand, will get involved with his Pop Warner team leadership. She can enjoy it because he enjoys it, and there are many ways she can pitch in. This is the essence of the aspiration stepping-stone on the LovePath. It is striving together, through mutual support, encouragement, and action, to accomplish each other's dreams.

When those dreams come into conflict? That's when we need to be more creative. My wife and I had to do that. When we finally began to understand what the core of our conflict was, that we had conflicting life desires and expectations, we talked about them until each of us understood our own life desire fully enough to explain it to the other. That took some time and a lot of self-reflection and probing.

You see, we didn't understand at first why we were always fighting when I came home from a trip or was about to go on one. She didn't like my going, but she liked the income my career provided. She didn't know why she became so irritable and touchy just before and after my trips. She would say she didn't like being alone, but she never asked me to stop traveling. Neither of us understood how deep her desire was that I be there every night. I worked hard as I traveled and thought her a nag when I came home to the turmoil. Our conflict was disguised in a hundred ways because neither of us had done enough self-examination to realize that we were at odds with what we truly wanted.

The solution started with each of us first figuring what was important to our own expectations about life, marriage, and family. Not only the *what*, but the *why*. Not only what actions or situations were desired, but what they symbolized. When we finally were able to figure that out, we sat down, affirmed each other's dreams, and talked about ways we could each get what we wanted. Together.

> *The solution started with each of us first figuring what was important to our own expectations.*

## THE ART OF COMPROMISE

The largest barrier I encounter when trying to teach a couple how to compromise is one or both of their fearing that if they give an inch, they will lose a mile. There's good reason for that fear; it's happened in the past. One person gets a small concession and uses it to gain larger concessions, especially through rhetoric and lots of persuading. Finally, the other gives in, not because they are happy with the result, but because they don't want to fight any longer. That kind of giving in isn't compromise, it's defeat. The more it happens, the more the person being defeated resents it and the more controlled they feel. So when I come along and start talking about compromise, all they see is that they are going to somehow lose again because their spouse will just use the new information to get what they want.

Allow me to emphasize: if either party loses—or feels the slightest sense of loss—it isn't a compromise, it is a victory and a defeat.

When compromise is accomplished, each party is happy with the result because it is a result they willingly decided upon and were not forced into. How do you do that? Because I'm a religious person, I would start any effort to find compromise by praying for wisdom. If you're a religious person, I urge you to do the same.

## Listen

After prayer (for those who pray), the first step is to listen. That's right, listen. Ask a few questions, not to probe, set up, or make the other feel dumb, but to really, truly understand two things:

- What it is that the other expects, or at the very least, desires
- Why the other expects or desires what they do

Sometimes when you ask what the other wants or why they want it, you'll hear, "I don't know." When that happens, don't become exasperated. Instead, accept that they don't know, but that with time and gentle examination it may be possible to know. Continue, not pressuring, but simply trying to understand.

When Alice and I grew to the point of asking and honestly answering those questions without arguing, we discovered things about ourselves and each other. Accomplishing that can change everything. It holds the possibility—maybe even the likelihood—of reframing the matter from a subjective view to an objective view. Therefore, talk.

Talk as long as it takes for each of you to understand the other's what and why to the point that you can feed it back to the other person and hear, "Yes, you've got it."

## Brainstorm

The second step is to brainstorm with abandon as to how each of you can fulfill your dreams or expectations, even if they appear contradictory. As we've worked with couples in crisis in our Marriage Helper weekend workshops, we've found that even the most contradictory of desires nearly always have a way of finding harmonious solution. As you might imagine, brainstorming isn't workable if each of you draws boundaries beyond what you really desire. If I had said to Alice that we could brainstorm, but that brainstorming could not include anything that changed my traveling, we would have gotten nowhere. If she had said it couldn't include anything that didn't have me being home for dinner every night, the same thing would have occurred.

By the time we began brainstorming, we each knew the core of what we wanted and were willing to allow changes in our current way of seeking our fulfillment. We trusted each other to the point that we knew we wouldn't end with a conclusion that benefited one and not the other. With that in mind and heart, we could brainstorm all types of possible solutions to our dilemma and neither stopped to fight over the other's potential ideas.

## Agree on a Solution

The third step is to agree on one of the brainstormed solutions and give it a try. By the way, that agreed-upon solution may not come with the first—or even the first few—brainstorming sessions. Sometimes it takes a while to find a solution that both are willing to try. The key word here is *try*. Don't feel that you've failed if the first potential solution doesn't work. That's part of life, no matter what we attempt. Some things work better on paper than they do in reality. If your solution isn't working, just back up one step and start again from there. If the next solution isn't working, then back up another step and start gently but thoroughly probing each other to see if perhaps you missed the what and why.

Don't jump back two steps at once. Only take one step at a time if something isn't working.

Alice and I did as described above and came to a solution that would take five or more years to complete. It gave me a way to gradually reduce traveling and replace that with another method of speaking that would allow me to be home most of the time. She got what she wanted and so did I. That solution

*If your solution isn't working, just back up one step and start again from there.*

took a while to devise, but as we worked on it, we noticed something. The very fact that we were trying to find the solution together, each wanting to support and fulfill the life desires of the other, changed our relationship long before the solution came to fruition. It changed as soon as we each started trying to understand and fulfill the other's life dreams. Therefore, the year it took to find the solution and the five years to implement the solution were not years of frustration, agony, selfishness, and unhappiness. Working on it together, with the mutual goal of fulfilling each other, put us squarely on the aspiration stepping-stone of the LovePath.

Since then I've helped many couples find ways to be creative in making their dreams cooperative rather than conflicting. Remember Bill and Yvonne from an earlier chapter? He wanted to see the whole country in his sports car; she wanted a well-furnished home and a family. These could seem like difficult dreams to reconcile, but the couple loved each other enough to make it happen. The turning point came when they sat down, talked about who they were, and understood where their dreams came from.

Their solution? Wait one more year before starting a family. During that year Bill would take a leave of absence from his job, get his car fixed up, and, during the summertime, take Yvonne on a three-month drive across America. During those hours in the car, they would turn off the music for a certain amount of time each day and simply talk— mostly about the family they intended to raise, God willing. They would see all the great sights, camping out when they could, just as Bill had always dreamed. Then they could look forward to a time several years down the road, when one or two school-aged children accompanied them on the same kind of trip. And, they hoped, after the nest was empty and a few dollars had been put away, they would sell the home, buy a Winnebago, and go in style.

Bill and Yvonne could see the path that lay ahead for them—an upward path, we might say. When they combined their dreams, they found they also combined their hearts. The journey is so much better that way.

You see, that's what aspiration is all about.

## A FINAL WORD ABOUT ASPIRATION

Everyone has expectations about life, marriage, relationships, family, career, and all sorts of other things. These expectations, when deep enough to be the dreams contributing to self-identity, worth, and those kinds of things, are extremely important to the person who has them. Going through the steps to compromise helps a great deal, and brings much-needed solutions. However, it doesn't necessarily settle all matters. Therefore, don't be frustrated or feel hoodwinked if solving one problem eventually leads to having to solve another. It's quite common. The good news is that it can be just as unifying, if not more so, to do it the second time as it was the first. Or the third. Or the fourth.

You get the idea. Don't dread the compromises you'll face in the future. Rather, enjoy them as a bonding element that lifts each of you to a higher level of relationship and a deeper level of love.

One more thing. Sometimes the problems that come in marriage are because a certain expectation was set in courtship that didn't pan out in marriage. Allow me to give a couple of examples.

Let's say that the woman grew up in a home where Dad was successful and provided everything his family needed. From that warm feeling, she fully expected and wanted that same kind of security and comfort in her own home when she grew up and married. She meets and falls in love with a wonderful young man. He is extremely bright, making straight As, and from those signs in his life and behavior she expected his intelligence and drive to evolve into a stable and successful career. So what happens if he drifts from job to job and can't seem to find his niche, creating financial strain and a sense of instability for his bride? Not only will she feel the frustration of an unfulfilled life desire, she will feel cheated. The promise she saw and experienced in courtship didn't pan out in marriage. In all likelihood she will begin to treat him with disrespect and begin to exert control in various ways in an effort to make him become successful, and the marriage will spiral downward.

In another example let's imagine that a couple was sexually active before marriage and their physical involvement was intense and passionate. That touches the man deeply because his dad always said he'd never be anything and that no one could ever love him. In his mind this intense sexual passion is proof of his lovability. His dream is to overcome the negative emotion from his youth. Neither he nor his wife will likely understand that the intensity of their courtship sex is driven mostly by limerence and that this emotional and psychological state won't last.

A couple years into their courtship they marry and, true to human nature, their limerence fades into companionship and bondedness. Where there once was passion in her eyes and an I-can't-wait-to-make-love-to-you impatience in her cravings, there are now jobs, household chores, even children to take her focus. How will he react? His dream is shattered. Inside he has to fight the mantra that his dad drove into him: "See, you aren't lovable. She doesn't want you any longer."

In this situation the husband is the one who will likely become controlling, trying everything he can to incite her passion to the level it once was and becoming angry if it doesn't happen or if he feels she is doing it just to appease him. He wants to be loved and reads her behavior as his being unloved—or unlovable.

Where do you think this marriage is headed? It, too, will spiral down unless each of them begins to understand the other's dreams and finds a workable way to fulfill them. But even if they can do that, does that mean that limerence will return? No, it can't. Still, this couple can find a way to a win-win compromise—if they'll work on it together.

What am I trying to tell you as I end this chapter? If you're single, be careful what your current actions promise about the future, even if you aren't aware that those promises are being made. If you're married, rather than being angry, frustrated, or intractable about your spouse's expectations, stop to examine how you may have promised through your actions—even if you had no idea you were doing it—that life was going to be a certain way. This isn't to make you feel guilty, but to help you understand why your spouse thought certain things were going to happen. Reframe it to see how you helped create that expectation and it may well help you be much more willing to compromise a way to fulfill it now.

*If you're single, be careful what your current actions promise about the future.*

## CHAPTER SUMMARY

*Once a couple reaches attachment, there are four things that can happen:*

- The couple may stagnate and maintain an existence together that isn't close.
- One or both may backtrack down the LovePath and lose their love.
- One may destroy the love of the other through attrition that comes from trying to control.
- They may take their love to greater heights as they spiral up through the step of aspiration.

*The key word for aspiration is* cooperate.

- Aspiration occurs when each understands his or her dreams or life desires and communicates them to the other, then both work to help the other fulfill those dreams.

*The way to compromise is to do the following:*
- Listen until you understand not only the *what* but also the *why*.
- Brainstorm without boundaries or limitations.
- Try an agreed-upon brainstormed solution.
- If the solution doesn't work, back up one step at a time until you find the right one.

# USING
# THE STEPS:
# AWAKENING

# LEARNING TO
# LOVE ANEW

*Alex and Annie* were both born in August. Some couples have a special song, others have a special restaurant. Alex and Annie have a special letter of the alphabet. In their home, you'll see the letter *A* in every style and color, in every kind of decoration. It was only natural for them to choose the first day of August for their wedding date. That became A-Day, and every year they would celebrate their anniversary and both birthdays with a big party for all their friends. Sixteen of those friends enjoyed the first annual A-Day bash during the year when Alex and Annie turned thirty. That was about the full capacity of the little bungalow that was their first home. Everyone agreed that Alex and Annie made quite-the-perfect couple. You could see the affection in their eyes. The two couldn't seem to stop holding hands, trading kisses, or rubbing each other's shoulders. The honeymoon endured.

Exactly ten years later, as Alex and Annie turned forty, the party was bigger. This was the tenth anniversary, after all. It was interesting to study the difference in the two. Both enjoyed the party, but they weren't quite so clingy or affectionate. That seemed fairly normal.

They were parents these days, and parents are usually a little less romantic and a little more grounded in the work of being a family.

At the party Annie hung out with the women in the kitchen. Her husband held court with the men in the family room, watching a baseball game on the television. Everyone had fun, but the party lacked a celebratory spirit somehow. There was no A-shaped cake this year, and by now Alex and Annie had stopped giving the funny little speeches that had detailed another year of marriage and paid tribute to each other.

When another ten years passed, and Alex and Annie turned fifty, everyone thought about the A-Day party and knew for certain there wouldn't be one. Alex and Annie had split four years earlier. They had been separated for eighteen months before finally getting the divorce. Most of their friends saw it coming, though there was no remarkable story connected to the split—just another couple that had fallen out of love and couldn't seem to coexist in the same house. The younger of the two kids spent weekends and a few holidays with Dad. The older one was in college.

*After hours of conversation, they knew they could forgive and accept each other.*

Everyone had forgotten the expired A-Day tradition by the time Alex and Annie were turning sixty. That's why so many people were surprised to receive the party invitation. Outside the special card was a beautiful letter *A* in golden script. Inside it read: "You are invited to help Alex and Annie celebrate the blessings of their marriage and sixty years of life." Immediately the phone lines were burning all over town. Everyone was trying to find out, was this a joke? What in the world was going on? It seemed that nobody had heard from either of the two divorcées lately. But you can bet that every single invited guest showed up right on time.

Alex and Annie met their old friends, hand in hand. They were tanned and smiling as they announced that they were just back from a second wedding and a second honeymoon: a trip around the world. Three years earlier, they explained, Alex had invited Annie to dinner. That evening and a series of subsequent dates were tightly held secrets, because neither of the two wanted the pressure of friends, family, or even their children complicating a fragile situation.

Both individuals had changed. Both had been thinking about their terrible pain, the cruelty of their words, and how things had gone so wrong. At first it was awkward to sit across the table from each other again. Each suspected that the meeting was a big mistake. Yet the next week, they met again, this time for a walk beside the river. By their third meeting, both had loosened up, and a flood of pent-up words and emotions began to tumble out.

Well, those are the basic revealed facts of the miracle. To the last moment, when Alex and Annie took the leap of faith and left together on an ocean cruise, they still weren't too sure they weren't out of their minds. They were married at sea. By the time they came home from their trip, there were no more doubts about a future together.

The sixtieth-birthday celebration was the quietest A-Day party ever. Everyone sat and listened, wide-eyed and all ears, as the couple took turns over dinner, telling about their trip. They were so . . . so *comfortable* together, quite a contrast to how nasty the divorce had been. Alex and Annie described what it was like to be together again, with so much pain behind them, so much emotional growth resulting from that pain.

They had traveled in Japan and Israel and Greece and Denmark, delighted with these cultures, equally delighted with each other. It was obviously hard to put into words, but the two of them had somehow reawakened their attraction. Only this time the attraction was deeper, because it was based on more information, more shared experience together, and it was grounded by more wisdom on their own parts.

Therefore, they had grown closer than ever before, partially because they had nothing left to lose. They had said and done the worst during the breakup and the divorce. After hours of conversation, they knew they could forgive and accept each other anyway. How wonderful it felt to let the bitterness go and forgive! They felt unburdened. The caring was deeper and more profound than when they had been young and madly in love. The attachment between them was more powerful than it had ever been. They finally understood how thoroughly they needed each other, how perfectly they completed each other. It seemed as if now, as they explored these countries together, they were learning even more about each other than they had in the beginning of their relationship.

Alex and Annie understood that every single one of us is a "culture" unto himself or herself—a culture with a special language, a special heritage and history, a special beauty all his or her own. You could spend a lifetime and not learn all there is to know about Japan; you could spend a lifetime and not penetrate all the mysteries of your own mate.

Finally, their shared desire for each to accomplish his and her life desires and dreams became the platform from which they knew they would grow deeper and deeper in love. And as that happened, their relationship went higher and higher. Alex and Annie were happy to begin that quest. They looked forward to growing old together, to taking care of one another as the last energies of youth slip away, and to having that special, profound companionship called love when they complete this life and come to the threshold of the next one.

Yes, Alex and Annie even talked about that! Who could have imagined such a thing at their first party, thirty years ago? They held each other's hands, allowed a tear or two to trickle down their cheeks, and spoke of their assurance that there must indeed be a heaven. After all, if love in this world could be so powerful, didn't there have to be another world waiting? Just as the air feels a certain way when rain is on its way, love makes us feel, deep in our soul, that its ultimate fulfillment is also coming.

The great news is that any relationship can grow deeper in love. Even greater news is that a couple can grow to have wonderful love for each other even if one or both of them no longer feel any love for the other. The greatest news is that it even works for those who have come to hate each other. Yes, they, too, can be wonderfully in love if only they take the LovePath seriously.

## A Word of Warning

I need to note here that too often a person wanting to maintain or re-establish a relationship with a lover who abandoned him will do the wrong thing. He tries to control the other, to somehow make her love him again. As we've pointed out throughout this book, control drives the other person away rather than bringing them closer to you. Clinging, demanding, threatening, manipulating, pleading, tolerating destructive behavior, participating in things that you know to be against your own morals, and all kinds of other bad things happen when one person tries to control.

I remember one wife who physically hurt herself thinking it would make her husband stay. Instead, it propelled him from her. I remember another wife who allowed her husband to bring his lover into their bed, thinking that would save their marriage. Though that seems to be an act of submission, it very much was an act to control. "If I do this for him, he'll stay with me. I can make him stay with me by doing this."

That never works.

Two things should never happen on the LovePath.

*Never allow another person to do bad things without consequences.*

First, never allow another person to do bad things without consequences. Enabling another's destructive behavior is NOT an act of love.

Second, never say you will be there whenever the abandoning or straying spouse decides to come back. There is nothing attractive or motivating about someone who allows the other to live as she wishes and then come back whenever she desires.

If your mate or lover has gone, don't cling, yearn, or live in limbo, thinking that things will be okay again only if he returns. Live your life with anticipation for what can be, not in mourning for what may have been.

Start with the PIES, for yourself! It is the best thing you can do for you. It may bring your lover back, but even if it does not, you need to do it for you.

Loving another does not *ever* call for the destruction or deterioration of oneself.

## BECOMING WHOLE

Love for another is only one aspect of life, but it's an essential one. The partners we choose will change us forever. The relationship we build will take on a life of its own, and once we have shaped it, that relationship will reach back and begin to shape us.

Some people are said to be "unlucky in love." That's an empty expression because love is never about luck. We create our own destiny based on how we walk the path. Having said that, it's true that there are some people who don't walk it well. Their failed relationships leave them sad and bitter. Perhaps you've known someone like that. There is a kind of pain in their eyes that never departs. There are others, like a few I've described in this book, who are rejuvenated and remade by the miracle of love.

I'm far from the first to make the following observation: love is the most powerful force in this world. It's strong enough that we will die for someone we love. It's also strong enough to completely reshape our lives.

After the love of a good person has done its work upon us, we find ourselves in a surprising new state. It's a kind of enlightenment, really. Our eyes are more open than ever. Our ability to listen and to care is elevated. We have more energy, more purpose, and we become more dynamic people. The change shows in us, so people cannot help but notice the difference. "Look at her," they say. "I believe she has fallen in love."

And that's only at the beginning. In the more advanced stages of the LovePath, the changes in us run far deeper than a smile on the face or a spring in the step. The LovePath has begun to make us whole. Think for a moment of the alternative. What is life without love? We tend toward self-absorption because there is no one to pull us out of ourselves. It's true that some people are more comfortable with solitude than others, but I'm convinced that every single one of us needs people in their lives—not just one to love, but a community to cherish. Those who go through life alone, keeping to themselves, are more likely to suffer from serious illness and to die sooner.

Therefore, as you walk the LovePath throughout your life, you will find many benefits you never anticipated, along with the priceless treasure of the kind of companionship I enjoy with my wife. You'll be more interested in the world around you. You'll also find yourself becoming generous in every way. Those who are blessed know the joy of blessing others, and they rejoice in the opportunity to give.

*The more deeply intimate you become with your beloved, the more you will find yourself involved with a wider circle of people.*

Remember the last scene of Dickens's *A Christmas Carol*, when Ebenezer Scrooge woke up on Christmas morning and engaged himself in a frenzy of donating to charities and sending anonymous gifts of turkeys for Christmas dinners? Love makes us joyful, and joy is something that cannot be contained. It overflows upon everyone around it. And there's a paradox here.

The more deeply intimate you become with your beloved, the more you will find yourself involved with a wider circle of people.

That seems like a contradiction, doesn't it? We think of two people deeply in love, looking for some island paradise where they can shut out the world. That impulse may take hold for a time, but ultimately love drives us into community involvement. We become great servants of our churches and our neighborhoods and our school boards. Nothing about your life will be the same, really. Your work will be radically different, filled with new energy and vitality. You will laugh more frequently and even be childlike at times, in the best sense of the word. There will be so many areas of life that interest and intrigue you; you will be much more curious. All of this is simply the way you were designed to be. It requires love to help us get there. Therefore, the Love-Path is part of the path of life—but that's a whole different book.

## ATTRACTION ON THE UPWARD PATH

Think about Alex and Annie. How in the world did they become attracted again to each other in midlife, after seeing the worst of each other in separation and divorce? Quite simply, they began to follow the LovePath, and for them that meant going back to the beginning. Though each had been hurt by the other, they started where love nearly always starts—with the first step of the LovePath: attraction.

It's not uncommon for couples to be drawn back together. I've seen couples divorced as long as ten years get back together, remarry, and make a great life. However, most of the time these "secondary cycles" of the upward LovePath happen with a couple already together, who have decided that what they *could* have is better than what they *do* have. Rather than stagnating, or even backtracking on the LovePath, they intend to grow even deeper in love.

The way to make that happen, as I've been sharing with you all along, is to follow the LovePath, to learn the art of being—and staying—in love.

It's never too late to be attractive to the other person. Similarly, it is never okay to feel that you no longer have to be attractive to the other person. This becomes quite clear to a husband or wife that comes to me asking how they can save a failing marriage. I tell them that to keep love alive and growing, we need to continually think of each step of the LovePath and do what it takes to fulfill the other person's need at that step. Just because a couple is married—even if they've been married many years—neither has the right to no longer be attractive to the other simply because they are currently attached. We continue to want our spouses to be physically, intellectually, emotionally, and spiritually attractive as long as we live. Though the way in which attractiveness is maintained or evaluated may change as we grow older, it is still there.

As we've seen, the attraction is deeper and fuller than simply a sexual one at this stage, but let's not make too many assumptions about sexual attraction as we grow older. A couple can be sexually active into their hundreds if they maintain good health. One of the unfortunate things I hear so often from a husband or wife is that they love their spouses more than ever and want to grow old together, but they don't want to make love to them any longer. The most common reason I hear is that their spouses have let themselves go and are overweight, not from a health condition but because they don't have enough discipline not to be. "Maybe we would still be sexual more than once in a blue moon if I could just be attracted again. I don't want a twenty-year-old stud nor do I want a plasticized fake body. I just want my spouse to look as good as he could look if only he cared."

*Make yourself as attractive as you can be at your age and in your situation.*

Are you seeing how this works? As long as you live, no matter what your current situation, follow the LovePath to make love grow. Continually cycle upward through attraction, acceptance, attachment, and aspiration. It is truly the path of love.

When one spouse either fears or knows that the other is abandoning the marriage, or that love has stagnated, I suggest starting at the very first step of being attractive again. Start with physical. Become as attractive as you can be at your age and situation in life. This doesn't mean looking like some model on the cover of a magazine. Not at all. It means doing what you can reasonably do to be and look healthy. Even if it has no effect on the departing spouse, it definitely has an effect on your own self-esteem, health, and welfare. I tell men and women alike to eat right, exercise, lose weight if they should, wear nice clothes, get a haircut, wear makeup, shave off the scruffy beard, or whatever works to accomplish both goals. What goals?

Simple. You want to make yourself as attractive as you can be at your age and in your situation so that (1) your spouse will be attracted to you again and (2) you can improve, for yourself, your self-image, health, and happiness.

What about the attractiveness of the mind? When a marriage is either dull or has gone as far as breaking up and the spouse wants to win back his or her beloved, one of my attractiveness suggestions is to join a book club, develop a new interest, or enroll in a class. Do something to keep your mind developing and learning. We don't do these things simply to entice someone in our direction; we do them because these actions make us better people. Particularly when we've lost at love, we begin to feel bad about ourselves—and lowered self-esteem makes us less attractive and much less happy with ourselves. We break that vicious cycle by building self-regard through both of these things: improving the physique and expanding the mind. We become more secure, more content, and therefore more attractive.

Reattraction can also be enhanced emotionally. I urge people to spend time with family or friends who love them and want them to be happy. I tell them that the worst thing they can do is sit at home with a book or TV because being alone nearly always leads to the dreaded pity party. That's when you sit around feeling sorry for yourself and become even more depressed. Get out, enjoy life, even if you have to make yourself do it. It is for your own mental and emotional health. Also, it often has quite an effect on one's partner, even if that partner is in the midst of leaving or has already gone. Remember, emotional health makes you attractive.

One of the interesting side effects of emotional health is that you become less clingy and more reliant on self, which often results in the other person seeing you as not needing them any longer. When that happens, you are no longer taken for granted. It's amazing how often, when the straying spouse realizes you can live your life happily without him, he's drawn back.

Don't forget to be attractive spiritually. Have you lapsed in your faith heritage? Whatever that belief set may be, I encourage people on the upward path to reconnect with their spiritual foundations. Again, we find ourselves growing on the inside as we do this. We benefit from the network of fellow seekers of faith. At the very least, find purpose and meaning for your life that supersedes you. We want to be like people we find spiritually attractive. While becoming spiritually stronger is one of the best things you can do for yourself, it also makes you very attractive to your lover, even if that lover is now with someone else.

There's nothing quite as wonderful as finding that we're falling in love all over again with the one we've loved all along. It seems like a small miracle—but it's part of the upward path. The neat thing about it is that even if it doesn't bring back our lover, if we've been abandoned, it gives us a wonderful sense of validation and self-worth. And it certainly makes you more attractive for any future partner you may join on the LovePath.

## ACCEPTANCE ON THE UPWARD PATH

In the original stage of acceptance, we began truly to care about the other person. You may remember that we spoke of coming to love the person rather than the picture of our beloved that we had in mind. Moving backward on the LovePath means coming to care less, sometimes without realizing it. We stop accepting certain realities about each other. The less we accept, the less we care. But what happens when we become reattracted? If we openly talk about the facts and feelings of our lives and find out we are accepted as we are now, that caring begins to move upward again.

Alex learned things he had never known about his wife, and some of it reframed how he thought about her. Both of them had become different people over the years. We all do, but Alex and Annie hadn't brought each other along on these changes, so in the beginning, there were sides of each other they truly did not know. Alex at forty-five, for example, was vastly different from Alex at twenty-five, because he became consumed by his career and by the pressure of providing the best home possible for his family.

Annie had never really thought about her husband in that light. As she learned about that side of him, she truly understood the forces that had been driving and worrying him. Her former resentment dissolved, then evolved into caring and became a desire to comfort and support.

As we grow in acceptance, we discover that we can even love each other especially for the warts, for those provide our opportunity to genuinely care. Annie had struggled with depression, and Alex had never tried to understand. Now he had compassion for her problem, he understood her moods, and he wanted to make things better. During years of separation and divorce, Alex lived in one home with nothing but his career-related pressure and remorse. Annie lived in another home with her depression and her own remorse. The time came when they no longer looked at each other and saw rough edges to keep them apart. Instead, they saw needs that each could help to fulfill. They each saw who the other could become with a little help.

That's how we take acceptance and caring to the next level in a relationship. In the beginning, we accepted each other as real people whom we were coming to know for the first time. Now it's different. We accept each other as changing people, moving targets for care and support. The personal needs are greater, and the challenges posed by life are more pressing. That makes our love stronger, for now we have a well-defined role. We want to help each other with those hurts. We care, and the deeper we come to know each other, the more deeply we will care.

*We accept the person rather than the picture, learning ever more about each other as we talk.*

However, this can only happen if we continue—or perhaps start—to allow each other to tell the truth. The real truth, even the parts that aren't pretty, about both facts and feelings. We accept the person rather than the picture, learning ever more about each other as we talk—really talk. Sometimes a person will say to me that his or her spouse isn't the kind that will ever talk much. I always reply, give them a chance. Ask questions and don't react negatively to what they say, even if you don't like it.

Validate thoughts and emotions even when you don't see it the same way. "I can see how you feel that," or "I can understand why you see it that way," goes a long way in encouraging the other to be genuinely open.

With time, even the most recalcitrant person—man or woman—will talk freely and openly when they know that they are being accepted and loved for the person they are rather than some picture that they have to present. And so the road goes ever onward, climbing to the higher level of attachment.

## ATTACHMENT ON THE UPWARD PATH

No one who attended that unexpected A-Day party ever forgot it. People sat quietly and listened to the story of a marriage that had been through the wars, one that had been left for dead and somehow rose again. You could see how real it all was: the faces of the husband and wife, the respectful and loving way they listened to each other, and the peaceful wisdom and contentment that came across in their voices. The maturity of their love made them more spiritually aware people, providing a shared meaning and purpose for life.

If you'll remember, *spirituality* is one of the four components of attachment. I've seen many couples reunite not because they were immediately in love again but because their beliefs and values led them to believe that they should. How do I react to that reasoning? I love it. I admire it. I encourage it.

A couple with shared spiritual beliefs, values, meaning, and purpose that will go through the other steps of the LovePath from attraction to aspiration will fall in love with each other no matter what has transpired before. Coming together, or staying together, because of spiritual reasons, even when no positive emotion exists otherwise, is a wise thing to do.

It only becomes miserable if that is all you do. Follow the LovePath with dedication, and the lack of love will develop into a wonderful love. Don't hesitate to let your spiritual beliefs lead that process when other parts of you are hesitant or resistant.

Another component of attachment is *respect*. From our story, it's obvious that Alex and Annie had a deeper respect for each other than ever before. This was true even though they had seen each other at their very worst. Their commitment to one another was tied to a deep regard for each other.

In attachment, we cultivate the relationship. The more we come to know each other, the higher our regard for the other, no matter what the flaws may be. We learn to respect rather than to control.

*Fulfillment* is another component. We find that the adventure of life is bound up with this companion, and that it's possible to enjoy the ride. Both Annie and Alex had physical, intellectual, emotional, and spiritual needs that longed to be fulfilled. In their new marriage, they purposely focused on each other's body, mind, heart, and soul. For Alex and Annie, travel brought out that sense of fulfillment. It was something they had always talked about doing, and now it was happening.

Most important, the upward path brings us to a sense of fulfillment in each other. This was the kind of love we always wanted, so long ago when we tied our futures together. No, neither of us has turned out to be perfect. Some dreams are unfulfilled, and some disappointments have been part of the path. The important thing is that we are not disappointed in each other. One of the most important elements of our dream has become simply to be together, because that is who we are.

Finally, there is the *passion* component. Yes, there is sex after youth. As a matter of fact, it's important. If you don't think so, go back and review the section describing how two people bond during sexual love. The more we are attached, the more we want to express our love physically. And the more we express our love physically, the more attachment we feel, even from a physiological perspective. It's a wonderful, self-perpetuating cycle. There is ample evidence that for many couples, the best lovemaking they will ever experience will be in their fifties and sixties.

But passion is more than sex. We want our lover to share in the important things with us. When anything new happens, we're immediately framing the words and phrases we'll use to tell our spouse about it. That's the real nature of passion, and sex is simply one expression of that. To continually grow in love, or to find love again, start with attraction, work on acceptance, and then, with intent and dedication, do what it takes to fulfill each other in your attachment, with respect, spirituality, and passion.

## ASPIRATION ON THE UPWARD PATH

Don't ever lose sight of the fact that aspiration is what spirals a marriage upward to its greatest heights. When you spend your lives helping each other fulfill dreams and life desires, you go beyond the selfishness that so often limits love. As we said in the last chapter, it may not be easy and it definitely calls for compromise. However, it takes you as a couple beyond the ordinary into a realm that only the most loving couples ever occupy.

*Aspiration is what spirals a marriage upward to its greatest heights.*

Each of you becomes fulfilled individually with the other as the biggest supporter. That personal fulfillment fills you and spills over into every aspect of your life, including your marriage and family. Share your dreams. Find the way to help each other make them come true. But do it together, not separately, and you will be as close as any two people on this planet have ever been. You deserve that. Make it happen.

## FINAL ENCOURAGEMENT

I hope that I've presented the LovePath simply enough and clearly enough that you understand it and can follow it. And I hope you're as excited as I am about learning the art of falling and staying in love. I also hope the LovePath becomes part of your vocabulary. I hope you ask yourself, and each other, questions such as these:

- Where are we on the LovePath? Are we growing, stagnating, or backtracking on the LovePath?

- Is either of us in danger of being on the LovePath with someone else?
- Am I confusing limerence with true love?

More than making these conceptual questions, occasionally self-examine to determine where you are on the LovePath, and be honest with yourself about whether you're growing, stagnating, or backtracking. Try to determine if you—not your lover, but *you*—are doing what you should to be as attractive to your spouse as you can be in body, mind, heart, and soul. Ask yourself if you are truly making it safe for your lover to be the person that he or she is rather than a picture that you either subtly or forcibly make them pretend to be. Regularly evaluate whether you are fulfilling each other, keeping passion alive, and demonstrating extraordinary respect and life-affirming spirituality.

Don't ever take it for granted that you are helping your spouse fulfill his or her dreams. Ask. Often. Ask with genuine concern and without a hint of selfishness, hesitation, or indifference.

From working with thousands of couples over many years, I can tell you this: the LovePath is the path to true love. Consciously follow it and your love life, and your lover, will be the best part of your life for a lifetime.

### CHAPTER SUMMARY

It is never too late to fall in love or to fall in love again. To keep growing on the LovePath, continue through all the steps, spiraling ever higher:

- No matter your age or the length of your relationship, continue to be as attractive as you can be at your age and in your situation in life—in body, mind, heart, and soul.
- As each of you changes over the years, keep open, respectful communication that allows each to know it isn't the picture but the person who is accepted.
- Throughout your life together, maintain your attachment by

continuing to demonstrate respect, fulfill each other, deepen passion, and grow together spiritually.

- Take your relationship to the highest levels through aspiration, sharing your dreams and life desires, and compromising so that each person wins.

# Group Discussion Guide

## Chapter 1: The Path to Love

1. How would you describe or define love?
2. What aspects of a relationship would you include in intimacy? (Things such as trust, openness, etc.) See if you can think of one that people might not typically think of.
3. What do you believe are the greatest obstacles to intimacy?
4. What would a couple need to do to develop deep levels of intimacy?
5. Reread Sternberg's description of *passion* (pages 12–13). How would you define or describe passion?
6. How could a couple deepen passion over their years together?
7. How do you think people view commitment in our society? In your opinion, how should they see it?
8. What could a couple do to deepen commitment?
9. If you are religious, what texts from Scripture can you think of that teach either intimacy, passion, or commitment?
10. If there were one thing from this chapter that you wish everyone in the world knew and understood, what would it be?

## Chapter 2: The Call to Closeness

1. Do you think it is fair that part of attraction is physical appearance? Give your reasons.
2. If you are married or in a relationship, what physical attributes attracted you to your mate? If you aren't in a relationship, what physical attributes do you most notice in potential partners?
3. How do you think physical appearance and condition affect relationships over time?
4. You read Joe Beam's view of intellectual attraction. What do you think is involved in intellectual attraction?
5. How do you think intellectual attraction (or the lack of intellectual attraction) affects relationships over time?
6. List as many ways as you can think of that one person may be emotionally attractive to another. Why are they attractive?
7. What do you think happens over time to emotional attraction in a relationship? What would you wish to happen?
8. You read Joe's view of spiritual attraction. What do you think is involved in spiritual attraction?
9. How could a couple deepen spiritual attraction over time?
10. If there were one thing from this chapter that you wish everyone in the world knew and understood, what would it be?

## Chapter 3: The Craving for Caring

1. How do people teach each other to lie in their relationship?
2. How would you describe or define acceptance?
3. Joe Beam states that acceptance is the most crucial aspect for falling in love. Why do you think that is true (or not true)?
4. Why is it so difficult for some to accept the thoughts, actions, or emotions of the one they love?
5. How is control the opposite of acceptance?
6. What should a person who feels controlled do to get the other person to stop controlling?

7. When should a person keep secrets from his or her spouse?
8. Joe gives three criteria for deciding whether you should tell a "secret." What are your thoughts about these criteria?
9. What would it take in a relationship for a person to feel that he or she could be completely open and honest about everything?
10. If there were one thing from this chapter that you wish everyone in the world knew and understood, what would it be?

## Chapter 4: Why We Fall Madly in Love

1. How would you describe limerence?
2. What bad decisions have you seen people make while in limerence? Give examples.
3. When is limerence good and when is it bad?
4. Discuss the thirteen characteristics of limerence. Which of these characteristics have you experienced personally or seen in another?
5. Discuss the three things that cause limerence to cease. Which have you experienced personally or seen in another with any of these characteristics?
6. Why is limerence not an actual step on the LovePath?
7. What does the expectation of lifelong limerence do to a relationship over time?
8. Why do you think that we are made to have limerence for only a relatively brief period of time?
9. What is the value of bonding over limerence?
10. If there were one thing from this chapter that you wish everyone in the world knew and understood, what would it be?

## Chapter 5: The Stage of Commitment

1. Why is attachment so important to a relationship?
2. Why is it crucial that a person actually believe and feel that the other respects him or her?

3. Give examples of how people demonstrate disrespect, whether they realize it or not.
4. How do the body, mind, heart, and soul characteristics in the fulfillment section of the attachment step differ from the body, mind, heart, and soul characteristics in the attraction step?
5. How would you describe or define *spirituality*?
6. How does mutual spiritual fulfillment affect a relationship?
7. Research shows that 20 percent of married couples in America have sex with each other ten times a year or less. Another 15 percent have sex twenty-five times a year or less. Why do you think this is the case?
8. How could couples change their relationship so that they each wish to have sexual union more often?
9. Explain how passion includes sex but is much deeper than just sex.
10. If there were one thing from this chapter that you wish everyone in the world knew and understood, what would it be?

## Chapter 6: The Dynamics of Difference

1. Which temperaments do you think are your strongest (the ones that best describe you)? Explain.
2. Which temperaments do you think are least like you? Explain.
3. If there is time available, have the group speak to each person giving their views of his or her temperament.
4. Discuss various compatibilities and conflicts that might exist in a marriage or relationship where the male is a commander and the female is a completer.
5. Discuss how those compatibilities and conflicts change in either nature or intensity if the female is a commander and the male a completer.
6. Discuss the compatibilities and conflicts that might exist in a marriage or relationship where one is a communicator and the other is a calculator.

7. In a relationship where temperaments collide or cause dissension, what things could the couple do to make the relationship more peaceful and fulfilling?
8. If a couple in the group is willing to illustrate from their own relationship how their temperaments collide, have them do so and then have the group brainstorm ideas the couple might use to handle those "collisions."
9. How could parents use understanding of temperaments to best parent each of their children?
10. If there were one thing from this chapter that you wish everyone in the world knew and understood, what would it be?

## Chapter 7: Relationship in Retreat

1. How do people who were once in love lose that love?
2. What are ways in which attachment weakens?
3. What are some of the reasons one person may stop accepting the other?
4. Use the LovePath model to explore and explain how affairs happen.
5. Joe lists several things he calls "nonsexual" affairs. What are your views about nonsexual affairs?
6. Joe modified the CAGE questionnaire used in alcohol abuse evaluation to one that he feels is applicable to relationships. Do you agree or disagree with his method?
7. At what point do you believe a married person "crosses the boundary" with another person? Why?
8. What are your views about one spouse forgiving and reestablishing a relationship with the other spouse who was unfaithful?
9. Joe says that any marriage can be saved. Do you agree or disagree? Why?
10. If there were one thing from this chapter that you wish everyone in the world knew and understood, what would it be?

## Chapter 8: The Challenge of Conflict

1. In this chapter Joe lists Dr. Frank Scott's categories of pain that lead to anger. Discuss each of these categories. Can you think of more?

2. Have you ever self-medicated your pain/anger? If so and if you are willing to discuss it, what was the pain and how did you self-medicate?

3. Joe writes that framing makes a large difference in how one handles pain and anger. What is your understanding of framing and how would it work?

4. Ask if anyone in the group is willing to speak about a pain/anger he or she has right now. If so, listen to the pain and then brainstorm ways that he or she might frame it differently to overcome the pain. (Be sensitive and understanding.)

5. Dr. Scott identifies three types of people when it comes to dealing with anger. Which are you and why are you that way?

6. How could a person use the concept of the "conflict circle" to change the next argument or disagreement with his or her spouse?

7. Discuss the Four Horsemen proposed by Dr. Gottman. Which have you done and how did they negatively affect the person they were directed at?

8. Why is forgiveness an act that is more for you than the person whom you are forgiving?

9. Joe lists three steps to forgiveness—two required and one optional. Do you agree or not, and why?

10. If there were one thing from this chapter that you wish everyone in the world knew and understood, what would it be?

## Chapter 9: The Fulfillment of Intimacy

1. Have the group discuss their understanding of the Aspiration step on the LovePath.

2. Have the group discuss their understanding of Attrition and how it takes one the wrong way on the LovePath.

3. Joe mentions stagnation, backtracking, and control as three alternatives that too often occur rather than Aspiration. Which of these have you witnessed and what was the effect?

4. Discuss the difference in overt control and covert control. Which do you think is worse and why?

5. If there are those in the group willing to be open with the following, ask them: If you can identify a dream or life desire you have, what does that dream or life desire symbolize or mean to you? Why is it important?

6. Joe lists three steps for reaching compromise. How effective do you think these steps would be in your marriage or relationship and why?

7. How do people somehow create an expectation in courtship of what marriage will be like, and then not fulfill that expectation in the marriage itself? Give examples.

8. What should a couple do when solving one problem leads to another problem? How do they keep that from stopping progress as they compromise?

9. Why is it crucial for each person to keep the promises he or she makes to the other?

10. If there were one thing from this chapter that you wish everyone in the world knew and understood, what would it be?

## Chapter 10: Learning to Love Anew

1. Joe states that a couple can keep spiraling up the LovePath for a lifetime, falling more in love over the years. Do you agree or disagree and why?

2. How does the Attraction step on the LovePath stay important throughout the life of a relationship?

3. How could each person ensure that he or she continues to become more attractive to the other over the years? Be sure to discuss Physical, Intellectual, Emotional, and Spiritual attraction—body, mind, heart, soul.

4. How does each person continue to grow in Acceptance of the other over time?
5. How can a couple continue to deepen their relationship by using the Attachment step?
6. How does passion change over the years? What would a couple do to make it more fulfilling than the passion they felt at the beginning of their relationship?
7. Why do you think that couples in their fifties and sixties often have the best sexual relationship of their lives together?
8. What do you think is the most important thing a person could do to help his or her mate reach Aspiration?
9. From these ten chapters, what is the most important thing that you learned for yourself?
10. If there were one thing from this chapter that you wish everyone in the world knew and understood, what would it be?

# Acknowledgments

*As always, my* sincerest appreciation to Philis Boultinghouse at Howard Books. For years she has taken my efforts and turned them into books that actually helped people. She is a remarkable and gifted person. Also, thank you to Amanda Demastus at Howard Books for always being on top of everything needed for this book and doing so with graciousness. Additionally, thanks to Karen Ball for her wonderful editing.

# Bibliography

Allen, J. *As a Man Thinketh: James Allen's Original Masterpiece*. Rockville, MD: Arc Manor, 2007.

Berger, A. R., and R. Janoff-Bulman. "Costs and Satisfaction in Close Relationships: The Role of Loss–Gain Framing." *Personal Relationships* 13, no. 1 (2006): 53–68.

Bingham, W. V. "Halo, Invalid and Valid." *Journal of Applied Psychology* 23, no. 2 (1939): 221–228.

Brown, R. L., and L. A. Rounds. "Conjoint Screening Questionnaires for Alcohol and Other Drug Abuse: Criterion Validity in a Primary Care Practice." *Wisconsin Medical Journal* 94, no. 3 (1995): 135–140.

Dixson, B. J., G. M. Grimshaw, W. L. Linklater, and A. F. Dixson. "Eye-Tracking of Men's Preferences for Waist-to-Hip Ratio and Breast Size of Women." *Archives of Sexual Behavior* 40, no. 1 (2011): 43–50.

Ewing, J. A. "Detecting Alcoholism. The CAGE Questionnaire." *Journal of the American Medical Association* 252, no. 14 (1984): 1905–1907.

Fisher, H. E., A. Aron, D. Mashek, H. Li, and L. L. Brown. "Defining the Brain Systems of Lust, Romantic Attraction, and Attachment." *Archives of Sexual Behavior* 31, no. 5 (2002): 413–419.

Furnham, A., M. Dias, and A. McClelland. "The Role of Body Weight,

Waist-to-Hip Ratio and Breast Size in Judgments of Female Attractiveness." *Sex Roles* 39, nos. 3/4 (1998): 311–326.

Gottman, J. M. *The Marriage Clinic: A Scientifically-Based Marital Therapy.* New York: W. W. Norton & Company, 1999.

Harley, W. F., Jr. *His Needs, Her Needs: Building an Affair-Proof Marriage.* Grand Rapids, MI: Fleming H. Revell, 2001.

Komisaruk, B. R., C. Beyer-Flores, and B. Whipple. *The Science of Orgasm.* Baltimore: The Johns Hopkins University Press, 2006.

McCarthy, B., and E. McCarthy. *Rekindling Desire: A Step-by-Step Program to Help Low-Sex and No-Sex Marriages.* New York: Brunner-Routledge, 2003.

McElroy, T., and J. J. Seta. "Framing Effects: An Analytic–Holistic Perspective." *Journal of Experimental Social Psychology* 39 (2003): 610–617.

"Oxytocin: It's a Mom and Pop Thing." *Science Letter*, September 7, 2010: 285. Expanded Academic ASAP. http://find.galegroup.com .ezproxy1.library.usyd.edu.au/gtx/infomark.do?&contentSet=IAC Documents&type=retrieve&tabID=T004&prodId=EAIM&docId =A236940202&source=gale&userGroupName=usyd&version=1.0.

Smedes, L. B. *The Art of Forgiving: When You Need to Forgive and Don't Know How.* New York: Moorings, 1996.

Sternberg, R. J. *Cupid's Arrow: The Course of Love Through Time.* Cambridge, UK: Cambridge University Press, 1998.

Tennov, D. *Love and Limerence: The Experience of Being in Love.* Lanham, MD: Scarborough House, 1999.

Thorndike, E. L. "A Constant Error in Psychological Ratings." *Journal of Applied Psychology* 4, no. 1 (1920): 25–29.

Wallace, A. "The Brain on Love: Scientists Are Closer to Understanding Why People Fall Head Over Heels for Someone." *Science World* 67, no. 7 (2011): 12–15.

# INTENSIVE WORKSHOP FOR MARRIAGES IN CRISIS

Marriage Helper is a turnaround weekend that will dramatically change your relationship with your spouse, regardless of what you feel for each other now—even if your love is fading or lost. We specialize in helping marriages facing difficulties such as:

- infidelity
- controlling spouse
- hurtful communication processes
- faded or lost love
- disrespect
- boredom
- different goals or aspirations
- inability to forgive

Any marriage can be saved! Think it's impossible? We know it isn't! It's a fact: any marriage, regardless of how bad it is now, no matter the problems being faced, can not only be salvaged, but both husband and wife can fall deeply in love again. It doesn't matter what you feel about each other right now—anger, bitterness, rage, hatred, or no feelings at all.

Our experience with thousands upon thousands of couples teaches us that there is a way—a methodology—that will turn around your marriage, stop the hurt, and rekindle the love that you had for each other back in the beginning.

For more information on this marriage-saving workshop, visit www.MarriageHelper.com or call toll-free (866) 903-0990.